Asking Better
QUESTIONS

Models, techniques and classroom activities
for engaging students in learning

NORAH MORGAN
JULIANA SAXTON

Pembroke Publishers Limited

To Charles Morgan and Christopher Saxton
whose being made the Unanswerable questions
easier to endure

Published in 1994 by
      Pembroke Publishers
      538 Hood Road
      Markham, Ontario L3R 3K9

Originally published in 1991 by Routledge as *Teaching, Questioning & Learning*

Canadian Cataloguing in Publication Data

Morgan, Norah, 1918-
  Asking better questions

Includes bibliographical references and index.
ISBN 1-55138-045-5

1. Questioning. 2. Teaching. 3. Learning.
I. Saxton, Juliana. II. Title.

LB1027.44.M67 1994   371.1'02   C94-931953-8

Cover Design: John Zehethofer
Cover Photography: Ajay Photographics

Printed and bound in Canada by Webcom
9 8 7 6 5 4

Contents

Acknowledgements

We are especially grateful to the following colleagues: Cecily O'Neill and Margaret Burke who read the earliest drafts and made some startlingly sensible suggestions which put us on the right track; Ida McCann, Teaching and Learning Project Officer, for her invitation to work with the Tasmanian teachers whose enthusiasm and insights got us started in the first place; to Madge Craig and Vicki Green for sharing their research and classroom expertise; and to Dr Francess Halpenny for her invaluable assistance at a critical moment.

We are grateful to the following for permission to quote material: the *Toronto Star* syndicate for an extract from 'Temagami' by Kathleen Kenna (8 December 1988); both McLelland & Stewart Publishers courtesy of the Lucinda Vardey Agency and A.P. Watt Literary Agents (on behalf of the estate of Margaret Laurence) for an extract from *A Bird in the House* by Margaret Laurence; Random House Inc. (© 1987 James A. Michener) for an extract from *Legacy* by James A. Michener; and to William Stafford whose poem 'Traveling through the dark' appears in *Stories That Could Be True* published by Harper & Row (1977). While every reasonable effort has been made to obtain copyright permission for the material used in this book the authors and publishers apologize if there are any omissions.

We are indebted to Jonothan Neelands, Paul Bidwell, Carole Tarlington and Linda Laidlaw for allowing us to make use of their teaching structures; and to our students and colleagues who let us test out the work on them and who never hesitated to refine and reshape our theory and practice with grace and humour. Joanne Smith and Kim Pelchat at the Resource Centre, Faculty of Education, Brock University, were infinitely helpful in answering our questions and asking others which we didn't know we needed to ask. Special thanks to Robert Tarling and to our editor, Helen Fairlie, who has always been there when we needed her.

Above all, we thank Ted Morgan who has undertaken the nurture and care of authors for the second time and refined the art to a degree of perfection hitherto unknown. What heights can yet remain?

Introduction

> Empowerment implies contributing to the shaping of society, rather than being subjected to the power of others. It goes beyond critical thought and includes a readiness to act with others to bring about the social conditions that one has chosen through a process of collaborative, critical inquiry. Action requires courage, but it also requires a possession of knowledge and skills necessary to change the situation – a classroom, school or any other area of human activity.
>
> (Berlak and Berlak, 1987: 170)

In any nation which works under a democratic system, it is understood that the power rests with its citizens. Elected representation and government are the responsibility of every member of society and each individual is responsible for monitoring the operation of government and for changing that representation when it no longer meets the needs of the society it is serving.

In a democracy, the voice of the minority has as much right as the voice of the majority to be heard and, for both, that right carries with it responsibilities: the responsibility of being able to see the issues clearly; to cut away the rhetoric and seductions of short-term advantages and to understand the implications; to give expression to concern through constructive action; and to be able to mediate individual concerns within the collective vision.

These responsibilities depend upon the skill of every member of society to ask the right questions: What is this really about? Whose values are being addressed? Who or what will benefit? Who or what will be diminished? What actions are possible? What am I prepared to give up? and so on. The ability to ask the right questions lies at the core of the democratic process.

The classroom has been described as the cradle of democracy and the teacher as one of the most influential nurturers of the democratic process. Those of us who are interested in education recognize the significance of questioning as the means by which teachers help students to construct meaning. We also know that the collective construction of action which gives voice to that meaning is dependent upon the students' skills in *asking* productive questions.

All teachers, however successful, are constantly seeking to improve their questioning skills. This book is offered in the hope that, by examining how we question, we will arrive at some answers which will generate richer classroom interaction and provide our students with opportunities to develop and practise that essential democratic skill.

WHAT IS THIS BOOK ABOUT?

This book is about:

- examining why teachers are not secure as questioners and why students are so often shut out of the questioning process;
- helping teachers to understand why questions are so important to teaching and learning in the twenty-first century;
- suggesting an uncomplicated way to classify the questions teachers need to ask in order to acquire information, build understanding and generate reflection; and
- offering models, techniques, activities and examples which promote better questioning by teachers and students.

The first section of the book examines the two structures which form the matrix of all educational processes: the structure for thinking and the structure for feeling. If you understand how these work you will be able to use them as guides both to evaluate what *has* happened in your classroom and to enable you to plan what you would *like* to happen. Most important of all, they help you to understand what is happening *as it is happening*. This, of course, has particular implications for questioning. Although you can plan one or two good questions, good questioning techniques come with the ability to ask the right question at the right moment, *inside* the give and take of classroom talk and activity.

The middle section looks at a simple three-part classification of general functions for questions: questions which tap into what is already known and which elicit a sense of responsibility towards the conduct of and approach to the work; those which build a context for shared understanding; and those which challenge students to think critically and creatively for themselves. Within this classification there are many kinds of questions which we present as a 'glossary of questions' so that you may see the wide potential of questions for generating thought and feeling.

In the final section of the book we concentrate on building questioning skills for teacher and students, suggesting techniques for posing questions and dealing with answers. We offer a variety of teaching stances for questions and for answers which will elevate language and encourage divergent thinking. We suggest roles and situations which will engage students as questioners and answerers and we provide practical exercises for developing these skills.

Each section is illustrated with an example lesson, drawn from our own experience or those of our colleagues and students. While some things have been synthesized for clarity and brevity, everything we describe throughout the text has been 'test-driven' in the real world of the classroom.

HOW TO READ THIS BOOK

This is not a linear text which requires the reader to complete a series of skill-testing questions before moving on to the next chapter. Useful though these may be, we would rather you exercise your own control and read in whatever way you choose. Of course, you may begin at the beginning and work your way through to the end but, on the other hand, you might prefer to 'go in' at the place where something catches your eye. Whether you simply leaf through the pages or check out the Contents, Index or Notes, whatever focuses your attention can provide an entry point from which you may move back and forth through the text as your interests and needs dictate.

Wherever possible we have talked about teachers and students but there are times when we talk about *a* teacher and *a* student. We follow the principle that the teacher will be referred to as 'she' and the student as 'he', unless a specific example dictates the gender.

Norah Morgan
St. Catharines, Ontario

Juliana Saxton
Victoria, British Columbia

'He that questioneth much shall learn much, and content much; but especially if he apply his questions to the skill of the person whom he asketh; for he shall give them occasion to please themselves in speaking and himself shall continually gather knowledge . . .'

Sir Francis Bacon (1561–1626)

Part I

Why the question?

Chapter 1

What seems to be the problem?

Let us . . . make the study of the art of question-asking one of the central disciplines in language education.

(Postman, 1979: 140)

In 1969 and again in 1979, Neil Postman suggested that questioning was as much a language art as reading and writing and he was 'astonished' that as such it continued to be neglected. 'In the development of intelligence', he writes in *Teaching as a Conserving Activity* (1979), 'nothing can be more "basic" than learning how to ask productive questions' (Postman, 1979: 140).

We, too, are astonished (to borrow Mr Postman's word) that, in the matter of question-making and question-asking, the message is still not getting through. There are a number of texts on questioning which are very useful (see Bibliography), a great many interesting articles and theses and, of course, Faculties and Colleges of Education do deal with questioning as a component of teaching methodology. But in everything we have read or seen or heard or experienced, the emphasis seems to be on theory and the theory of practice rather than upon the everyday practicalities of classroom interaction, that is: the active 'what is happening' engagement of teacher and students with the subject.

We work with classroom teachers, teachers who supervise teaching practice in their classrooms and with teachers-in-training. They know that whatever the plan, strategy or technique, effective teaching depends primarily upon the teacher's skill in being able to ask questions which generate different kinds of learning. They are aware that their questions do not draw on the wide learning possibilities inherent in the subject material and, at the same time, they recognise that their questions lack the sort of vitality that challenges students to approach their learning creatively.

If you are a classroom teacher, you may recognize, one or two of the following quotes as part of your experience:

'We had a wonderful discussion in class today. I've no idea why it went so well.'

'You'd think they'd be interested in the rain forest situation after that super film. But could I get the discussion going? No way! They sat around like they'd been hit on the head!'

'I asked some really "higher-order questions" to get them thinking. I got nothing but "low-level" answers!'

'My problem with asking questions is that once they get going, they won't shut up. I really don't have that kind of time.'

If you are a teacher-in-training or a teaching practice supervisor, are any of these familiar?

'Ms Young will never be an asset to the teaching profession until she gains more experience in questioning.'

'John is a lovely person who loves kids and will be a wonderful teacher when he improves his questioning skills.'

'I think I was asking some good questions today but my supervisor is concerned that I was losing control. How do I convince her that I wanted the students to talk amongst themselves as well as with me?'

'The problem with Mr Auld is that I get so interested in what he's teaching that I wish I was part of the class. I want to answer his questions instead of analysing them!'

Of course, we are, or have been, students. Do any of these ring a bell?

'Ms Brown only asked one question today and we kicked it around for the rest of the class – in fact, we're still talking about it.'

'Why should I bother to tell him the answer when he already knows it?'

'She knows I know the answers, so she never asks me anymore.'

'The teacher asks us questions to make us look stupid so he can show off what he knows about everything.'

Apart from the familiarity and, for some of us, a nostalgic recognition that 'the more things change, the more they remain the same', what could these quotes be telling us? Perhaps they are telling us that:

- A good question is seductive; like a work of art, the response it generates is for enjoyment, not analysis!
- If you don't know what makes a good question, it is difficult to recognize one.
- Those who understand the value of questions do not know how to make questions relevant to their students' experience.
- Teachers often do not realize, or cannot accept, that the consequence of a good question is that it generates a silence filled with thought which leads to talk.
- Teachers are often worried by the consequences of *good* questions

because of the noise of vital talk; the perceived lack of control (perceived by whom – the Principal? self? students?); the inability to handle misinformation as it circulates in the talk; the loss of time from curriculum coverage and/or the difficulty of involving those students who are not overtly participating.

- Many teachers are not aware of the significance of peer talk to the learning process.
- Teachers tend to lose their confidence when they find themselves in the same position as their students: pursuing a question which has no one right answer.
- Teachers become uncomfortable when dealing with material that cannot be measured in traditional ways.
- Teachers do not recognize that they are using questions as part of their discipline and control agenda.
- Some teachers misunderstand the nature of education. They perceive knowledge as immutable and learning as knowing the right answer.
- Quantity experience is not the same as quality experience: the more questions you ask does not make you a better questioner, it only helps you to ask more questions in a shorter time!

To sum up, what these quotations are revealing could be an ignorance of the art of questioning; a reluctance, perhaps, to break from the traditional structure of the teacher/student relationship; a misunderstanding of the nature and purpose of classroom discourse and the intrinsic value of that discourse to the learning process.

HOW DO WE VIEW THE STUDENT IN THE EDUCATIONAL PROCESS?

We all know that education is concerned with the development of the 'whole' student and, like Caesar's Gaul, the whole student is divided into three parts:

1 What the student thinks and knows. (The Cognitive Domain)
2 What the student feels about what he thinks and knows. (The Affective Domain)
3 What the student does as a result of his knowledge, thoughts and feelings. (The Psychomotor Domain)

No part is more or less important than another and the overriding educational goals in all curricula are to show that the whole is greater than the sum of its parts. Take, for example, this goal from an Ontario curriculum policy document (Ontario Ministry of Education, 1988: item 2 of 13): 'To help each [sic] child to develop resourcefulness, adaptability and creativity in learning and living.' If you accept that students, like everyone else, are sentient beings and that you cannot separate feeling from thinking and doing, then you may have little difficulty in recognizing a good question and what makes it work. Everything that goes on in the classroom, but most specifically in good questioning, must be presented in such a way that it 'connects' with the students at both an intellectual and a *feeling* level. Teachers can teach until they are 'blue in the face' but learners will not learn unless they *want* to learn. This is something everyone has always known.

So why is it that schools tend to concentrate on the cognitive and psychomotor development of their students and leave the affective to educate itself? A fact is a public thing; knowledge is public. Both a fact and knowledge can be shared and objectively measured (for the most part). But one's emotions, attitudes, values and beliefs are regarded as personal and therefore, private. Such things can only be assessed subjectively, if they can be measured at all.

It is not surprising that traditionally there has been no place for private matters in the educational system. This is perfectly understandable. The nineteenth-century view of society was one in which everything had its place. Matters of the spirit belonged in the church, domestic affairs in the home, business in the workplace, 'book-learning' in schools and universities, sex in marriage and feelings locked away in the heart.

The late twentieth-century view is very different. Today teachers in elementary and secondary schools are required, as a result of changing societal patterns and the true universalization of education, to be responsible for domestic, moral, career and health education. Many schools, however, still retain a nineteenth-century designation as places where only factual knowledge is acquired and where the affective domain is effectively ignored (Egan, 1987: 33–7).

There have been scholarly studies which refer to the importance of the affective domain but most educational practice still appears to be influenced by the traditional tenet that the student is a sponge to soak up information, a *tabula rasa* to be written upon by the teacher, a jug to be filled with knowledge. Certainly psychologists in general, as James Britton points out, have 'traditionally concentrated upon cognitive organization and tended to regard emotion as itself disorganized and *possessing a disorganizing influence*' (italics ours) (1970: 217). Such a situation is no longer tenable because today we know a great deal more about the effects of the emotions on performance.

It has been recognized that a positive feeling can enhance physical and mental prowess; an inviting atmosphere can promote school success; a sense of self-esteem is evidenced when students can see that they *'own'* their learning (Purkey, 1978). 'Reluctant' students who are encouraged to become active participants in classroom interaction have a greater chance of becoming responsible and vigorous learners (Hannam, *et al.*, 1977).

WHAT IS A 'VIGOROUS LEARNER'?

The traditional view of participation has suggested that students are in the passive mode, that their participation involves taking in, absorbing, being acted upon and giving back without additions and elaborations. Of course, this type of participation has its place in the teaching/learning interaction and there are times when it is effective, as long as it does not strangle initiative nor inhibit the contributions of the learner.

In our view of participation the students are in the *active* mode: not only taking in, absorbing and being acted upon but working energetically, acting upon their initiatives, acting upon others, asking questions and understanding that they have the right (and the responsibility) to contribute their ideas, experiences and feelings about the content and procedures of the lesson.

Effective teaching depends upon recognizing that effective *learning* takes place when the students are active participants in 'what's going on'. And for effective teaching and learning to occur, teachers must structure their teaching to invite and sustain that active participation by providing experiences which 'get them thinking and feeling', 'get the adrenalin flowing' and which generate in students a need for expression.

We do our students a disservice if we pay attention only to two-thirds of the whole person; we mislead ourselves if we think we can educate only by considering the intellect and we limit the power of learning if we regard teachers solely as transmitters and students solely as receivers in classroom interaction.

We believe that it is questions from both teachers *and* students that have the power to generate vivid ideas, spur the imagination and incite both teacher and student into a shared, creative learning experience.

There are, of course, implications in all of this:

- Effective questions generate in students thought and interest in making answers.
- Thoughts take time to formulate.
- Ideas need to be expressed and tested out.
- To be an effective questioner you will have to develop:
  - the patience to wait for answers to be formulated,
  - the skill of listening so that you will know how to respond,
  - the finesse to 'send the ball back' in such a way that learning is perceived by your students as a dialogue in which everyone's thoughts, feelings and actions are important elements for collective and individual understanding.
- As the classroom becomes an exchange for the expression of ideas, you will have to adjust your teaching style, your subject coverage

expectations, your assessment techniques and the way in which you go about your planning.

● Your position in the classroom will change as your students come to see you not only as someone with answers but also as someone who, like them, is seeking answers; someone who would rather have a classroom full of unanswered questions than unquestioned answers.

Before you throw up your hands, throw away this book or think that you will have to throw out all your strategies and techniques and start over – stop! We are not talking new philosophies, new methodologies or clean slates but rather a transformation of what you already know and practise into something which we hope will be more useful and more valuable for you and your students.

We begin by examining the structure of 'knowing' (or 'cognition') as it has been applied to the theory and practice of questioning. We do this because we know that this is something with which you are familiar and because it is important to build on what is known.

Chapter 2

A question of thinking

All our knowledge results from questions, which is another way of saying that question-asking is our most important intellectual tool.

(Postman, 1979: 140)

When we consider the development of thinking skills we turn for guidance to what is commonly known as 'Bloom's taxonomy'. In fact, the full title is *The Taxonomy of Educational Objectives: The Classification of Educational Goals, Handbook 1, Cognitive Domain* by Benjamin S. Bloom and David R. Krathwohl. The significance of the authors' work in clarifying the processes of logical thinking is undeniable and their contribution to education is considerable. To summarize, this taxonomy suggests that you cannot value or judge something until you (a) know the facts, (b) understand the facts, (c) can apply the facts, (d) can take the facts apart and (e) put the facts together in such a way that new perspectives are revealed (Bloom and Krathwohl, 1965).

Everything we have read about questioning tends to imply that questions, because they generate thinking, should follow the same hierarchical structure from the simple (recall) to the complex (evaluation). We believe that such a practice has resulted in distorting the place of questioning in teaching for a number of reasons. Simple factual recall questions are often not very interesting ways of beginning an inquiry; they are not 'attention-grabbers'. It is foolish to suppose that asking a simple question generates only simple thinking. 'Is the sun shining?' could cause your students to think in all sorts of different ways, particularily if the answer is 'yes' and they are wondering if you've gone blind or are merely trying a coy way of introducing a science lesson! Questions should spring from interest on the part of the teacher and of the student, and a structure which *dictates* the process inhibits the natural action of inquiry. The following example should demonstrate what we are talking about.

Here is a young teacher in a rural township in Australia, earnestly setting out a series of questions which will explore and develop her primary students' understanding of 'cities'. You will note how carefully she has followed the structure of 'Bloom's taxonomy'. She has invested a good deal of time and thought on her lesson plan because she hopes to be able to use it many times during her teaching career![1]

Her plan is to show a big poster of a busy harbour scene in New York City. These are the questions she will ask:

Question 1. *(Knowledge)*
    What do you see in this picture?
Question 2. *(Comprehension)*
    What do we call places like that?
Question 3. *(Application)*
    Do you know of any other places that look like this picture?
Question 4. *(Analysis)*
    Why are there so many policemen in the picture?
Question 5. *(Synthesis)*
    What if there were no policemen?
Question 6. *(Evaluation)*
    Would you rather live in a city that size or in a small town? Why?

When she asked the first question, a student replied, 'It's a picture of New York after a robbery. I wouldn't want to live in that dangerous city.'
Well? How would you fill in the next thirty minutes?
Suppose she had started out by asking the following question, which is simply her 'evaluation' question (6) rephrased?

'I wonder how our lives would be different if we lived here?'

Might she not have satisfied her lesson objectives and generated a more satisfying discussion for everyone?

As a structure, the taxonomy is not (nor was it designed to be) a constructive way of planning and asking questions. Bloom and Krathwohl's research is about *knowing* and as such is a very useful guide for seeing how we set thinking into action through questions.

WHAT IS THINKING?

There are many words which describe the ways we think, for example, the list from the New South Wales Education Department (1978):

Connecting	Contrasting	Rehearsing	Inducing
Arguing	Projecting	Testing	Approximating
Convincing	Questioning	Clarifying	Selecting
Generating	Reconciling	Reflecting	Deducing
Analysing	Suspending	Judging	Generalizing
Capitulating	Wondering	Disrupting	Alluding
Relating	Rejecting	Cooperating	Solving
Composing	Hazarding	Synchronizing	Matching
Retracting	Modifying	Harmonizing	Probing
Associating	Including	Speculating	Eliciting
Sequencing	Inventing	Contradicting	Soliciting
Suggesting	Extending	Assimilating	Recalling
Sorting	Accommodating	Empathizing	Calculating
Imagining	Proving	Compromising	Formulating
Comparing	Hypothesizing	Refuting	Valuing
Intuiting	Refining	Internalizing	
Predicting	Improving	Abstracting	

Some words mean almost the same thing (e.g. recalling and remembering), and others describe quite different ways of thinking. For instance, calculating is not the same as formulating, reasoning is different from imagining and judging is, when you think about it, not quite the same thing as evaluating. Just as there are people who have lived their whole lives using only a very limited vocabulary so it is possible to live within a narrow lexicon of thinking skills. But if you are in the business of educating, the mandate requires you to provide more than 'just enough to get by on'.

The more opportunities the teacher gives students to think about the same thing in different ways and different things in the same way, the more agile their minds will become. So when the teacher is planning questions or is involved in dialogue with her students there are always two things she is considering:

1. What kind of thinking is this question generating?
2. How will the question help students engage in and with the material?

WHAT KIND OF THINKING SKILLS ARE EXERCISED BY WHAT KINDS OF QUESTIONS?

To illustrate, we have chosen to use a simple source with questions formulated according to Bloom and Krathwohl's categories. The questions are geared to two different age groups – primary and secondary – and you will notice that the same question can often be asked of both groups. We have selected some answers to illustrate the variety of thinking that one question can generate. And because we believe that thinking cannot be disassociated from feeling, we ask at the end of each section a question designed to help you reflect on how students might be engaging with the material.

Source:

An illustration accompanying the nursery rhyme:

Little Boy Blue, come blow your horn,
The cow's in the meadow, the sheep's in the corn,
Where is the boy who looks after the sheep?
He's under the haystack, fast asleep.

Teaching unit: (Primary):   Environmental Studies: 'Children
                                everywhere'
                 (Secondary):   Social History: a study of children
                                in Victorian times.

(*Note:* This nursery rhyme was only one of a number of sources used in teaching these units.)

Teaching objective: To see our own situation more clearly as a result of
studying our past.

1. Questions which draw upon knowledge (Remembering)

Do we want our students to tell us what they already know through what
we have taught them, what others have taught them (teachers, friends,
parents, etc.), what they have perceived and/or experienced for themselves?
If the answer is 'yes', some of the thinking skills are:

recalling   remembering   recognizing   recollecting   defining
identifying

The question is often characterized by such key words as:

who?   what?   when?   where?

Question (Primary): 'In this picture, what is the colour of the boy's coat?'
Answers: 'Blue.'
                    'Sort of blue.'
                    'Bluey-green.'
Question (Secondary):   'Where would you find a haystack today?'
Answers: 'In the fields.'
                    'In barns.'
                    'Do we still have them?'

What in these questions might make you want to answer them?

2. Questions which test comprehension (Understanding)

Do we want our students to demonstrate that they understand what they
know through negotiating what is known into different patterns of
information? If the answer is 'yes', some of the thinking skills are:

rewording   rephrasing   comparing   explaining   interpreting
describing   illustrating   associating   differentiating

The question is often characterized by such phrases as:

what is meant by?   can you rephrase?   can you describe?
what is the difference?   what is the main idea?

Question (Primary): 'Can you describe his coat in your own words?'
Answers: 'His coat is the colour of the sky.'
          'It looks just like Mary's coat.'
          'It is a funny sort of jackety-thing.'

Question (Secondary): 'What is the difference between the appearance of

the shepherd in the picture and a shepherd today?'
Answers: 'I don't think there is much difference.'
'Do shepherds carry crooks today?'
'Shepherds today are usually grown men . . . and women,
too.'

What intrigues you about these questions?

---

3. Questions which require application (Solving)

Do we want our students to be able to select, transfer and use information and generalizations to complete a task through taking what they have already learned and applying it to other situations?
   If the answer is 'yes', some of the thinking skills are:

problem-solving   exampling   classifying   selecting   transferring
applying   hypothesizing   relating

The question is often characterized by such phrases as:

whom would you choose?   what would happen if . . . ?
if . . . how can . . . ?   what examples . . . ? how would you . . . ?

Question   (Primary and Secondary): 'Do you know someone like
Little Boy Blue?'
Answers   (Primary): 'Mary has a coat the same colour.'
'My brother, he sleeps a lot!'
'My friend lives on a sheep farm.'
Answers   (Secondary): 'I saw something on TV about child labour in
third world countries.'
'Remember the night watchman who fell asleep and the
bank was robbed?'
'My cousin walks dogs when their owners are away.'

This is a simple question but it seems to evoke a different kind of response from the previous categories. What might account for this?

---

4. Questions which encourage analysis (Reasoning)

Do we want our students to be able to support their arguments and opinions through organizing ideas into logical patterns of understanding? If the answer is 'yes', some of the thinking skills are:

analysing   determining the evidence   drawing conclusions
reasoning logically   reasoning critically   inferring   ordering

The question is often characterized by such words or phrases as:

why?   what if . . . ?   what was the purpose . . . ?   is it a fact that . . . ?
can we assume that . . . ?

Question   (Primary and Secondary): 'Why might he have fallen asleep?'
Answers   (Primary): 'He was sick.'
             'He was lazy.'
             'He'd stayed up too late watching TV.'
Answers   (Secondary): 'He probably had another job at night.'
             'Kids in those days weren't very well fed and they slept,
             sometimes, six to a bed.'
             'He was counting his sheep and just fell asleep!'

> What is there about this question which prompts this variety of
> answers?

5. Questions which invite synthesis (Creating)

Do we want our students to construct a connected whole from separate
elements through expressing original and creative ideas? If the answer is
'yes', some of the thinking skills are:

originating   integrating   combining   predicting   designing
developing   improving   reflecting   supposing

The question is often characterized by such phrases as:

how could we/you . . . ?   how can . . . ?   what if . . . ? I wonder how . . . ?
do you suppose that . . . ?

Question   (Primary): 'I wonder how he will explain to the farmer how the
           cow got into the corn?'
Answers: 'I think he should tell the farmer the truth.'
           'I'd say someone left the gate open . . . after all, they could have.'
           'He was away looking for a little lamb that was lost.'
Question   (Secondary): 'I wonder how it is possible to solve the problem
           of students having to hold a job while they are still in school?'
Answers:

'I wonder what would happen if they passed a Student Labour
Law so that no one under eighteen could hold a job?'
'Maybe we could go to school for a semester, then take off a
semester to earn money. I wouldn't mind that!'
'The Family Allowance cheque should be paid directly to us
once we enter High School.'

> What kind of feelings generated by these questions might lead to these answers?

6. Questions which promote evaluation (Judging)

Do we want our students to consider the values implicit in their thinking through looking at evidence and establishing criteria? If the answer is 'yes', some of the thinking skills are:

summarizing judging defending assessing arguing reasoning appraising criticizing appreciating selecting deducing deciding priorities

The question is often characterized by such phrases as:

which is better?   would you agree that . . . ?   would it be better if . . . ?
what is your opinion . . . ?   were we (you, they) right to . . . ?

Question   (Primary): 'Does it matter if he falls asleep if no one ever finds out?'
Answers: 'I don't think he'd feel good about it.'
'I don't think it matters . . . well, maybe it might . . . '
'He'd get found out anyway, 'cause the cow's in the corn!'
Question   (Secondary): 'Would it not be better if the Government took over all the financial responsibility for parenting?'
Answers: 'They'd certainly expect some sort of return for their money.'
'Don't they do that in Israel . . . on the kibbutz?'
'It would have to begin with the licensing of couples who want to become parents.'

> We wonder if asking students to make judgements gives them a sense of control over their learning?

REFLECTION

Some of the answers here demonstrate different kinds of responses from those the teacher had in mind and this may raise a few questions of your own. For example, the first answer to the Primary 'synthesizing' question would appear to be an answer at the 'evaluation' level.

Does it matter? No. You cannot *control* thinking; your job is to *generate* thinking.

You will note that a number of answers are in the form of questions. This suggests that in a comfortable classroom, students are prepared to ask for facts when they need them; if they aren't sure of them; or if there is something in their own experience which raises a question in their minds, for example, *'On the kibbutz?'* If teachers confine themselves to questioning from the so-called 'simple' (knowledge) to the 'complex' (evaluation), they may waste a lot of time – most students will ask if they don't know.

Can you imagine being in a class where the teacher initiates the above lesson by asking first:

'What is a haystack?'
'What is a meadow?'
'What is a horn?'

Answer: 'ZZZZzzzzz.'

If you like running a tight ship where you are in command because either you ask questions to which you know the answer or the answers your students give you won't interfere with what you know, you will tend to question within the first three of 'Bloom's' categories which are described as 'lower-order'.

Does that mean that a 'creative' teacher should never use the kind of questions which fall into the first three categories?

No, of course not. They're important when they *need* to be asked but you don't have to follow a particular schema which cannot take into account your students' background, experience and engagement with the material.

Many of us have problems with the last three or 'higher-order' categories (analysing, synthesizing and evaluating) for any number of reasons. For example:

- The questions present opportunities for expressing many divergent views.
- They offer opportunities for the class, or one or two students, to 'take over'.
- The class can split into factions and argue amongst themselves.
- You can lose the focus.
- It's hard to know whether students are being 'smart-alecks' or if they are working at a serious level of thinking *('He was counting his sheep and just fell asleep')*.
- Students can introduce things about which you know little or nothing.
- Discussion can move to a topic or aspect of a topic with which you are not comfortable.
- There are students who are left behind or left out.
- Sometimes the discussion will be unproductive, repetitive or seen as an opportunity for personal monologues which are irrelevant.
- It is difficult to wrap-up, bring to a conclusion or even just 'stop'.
- You are intimidated by the fact that these last three categories are often referred to as 'higher-order'.

Is this really as bad as it sounds? No, of course not! Like chairing a meeting or running a discussion, you have to keep in mind your focus and know *why* you asked the question(s). If, as a classroom teacher, you can visualize these apparent difficulties in a positive light, what do you 'see' and 'hear'? You see and hear students actively engaged in their learning, their minds 'ticking over' because you have aroused their interest and they are involved to the extent that they are taking responsibility for maintaining their engagement. Just sit back and keep your eye on which way the wind is blowing, the tides are running and what time you are due in port. Above all, try not to dip your oar into the water too often!

Why don't we just stick with 'Bloom' or any of the adaptations of 'his' taxonomy; they've been around a long time? You *can't* separate knowledge from feeling. Students and teachers bring their experiences and feelings into the classroom and those are vital components in the process of thinking. 'The real danger it seems to me,' wrote James Britton (1970: 217), 'lies in imposing a disjunction between thought and feeling, between cognitive and affective modes of representation. . . . We need to recognize the value and importance both of discursive, logical organization and at the same time, that of undissociated intuitive processes. . . . '

In the next chapter we will look at a structure which focuses on the place of feelings in teaching and learning. As the taxonomy of 'knowing' is a guide for generating thinking, so the taxonomy of 'feeling' is the guide for generating students' engagement with the material to be studied. Any fears, Graham Little (1983) points out, *that the Affective indulges emotion without cultivating knowledge and intellect would not appear to be supported by any . . . findings.*

And so reassured . . . onward!

Chapter 3

A question of feeling

Learning has to be felt for it to be effective . . . . It is this essential feeling level that is often either not recognized or ignored by teachers. Only when work is at an experiential feeling level can a change of understanding take place.

(Bolton, 1979: 31)

Children are by nature, smart, energetic, curious and eager to learn . . . . They learn best when they are happy, active, involved and interested in what they are doing.

(Holt, 1973: 2)

In the teacher/subject/learner negotiation, students are often more effective 'readers' of the teacher's emotional engagement with them and the material, than the teacher is of the students' emotional engagement with her and the material. Students may not understand what the teacher is talking about but they are always aware of the emotional sub-text. It has not occurred to them to separate thought from feeling and yet, as we have pointed out in the previous chapters, education has been attempting to do that for a very long time.

Learning springs from curiosity – the *need* to know. A good teacher capitalizes on that innate feeling by attracting, maintaining and satisfying the attention of learners while, at the same time, giving them something worthwhile to think about. It is the learners who actively go about the business of learning. This appetite for learning is very much like the appetite for food. The first question comes from the one who is hungry, 'What's for dinner?' The job of the cook is to provide a meal which is attractive and nutritious and then to stand by offering more when it is needed, suggesting items which might have been overlooked and providing an ambience which encourages digestion. But it is not the cook who picks up the knife and fork and eats. It is this active engagement of learners with their 'food for thought' with which we are concerned here.

Professional teacher training concentrates on the cognitive and the physical because they are both capable of measurement and observation. The study of feeling, as the *Encyclopaedia Britannica* (1962: 144) points out, is 'complicated by the fact that the event being perceived is *not open for direct inspection by others.*' Despite this apparent difficulty, teachers (if the quotations at the beginning of this chapter have validity) must pay attention to the fact that their students have emotional lives. Effective teaching and learning can *only* occur when teachers recognize that thought is unavoidably harnessed to feeling and when they know how to read the signs of that feeling engagement.

Anyone who is a teacher or who has been a student knows that there are different levels of involvement in any learning experience. We have identified these degrees of involvement as:

Interest: being curious about what is presented;

Engaging: wanting to be, and being involved in the task;

Committing: developing a sense of responsibility towards the task;

Internalizing: merging objective concepts (the task or what is to be learned) with subjective experience (what is already owned) resulting in understanding and therefore ownership, of new ideas;

Interpreting: wanting and needing to communicate that understanding to others;

Evaluating: wanting and being willing to put that understanding to the test.

These levels of involvement we call the 'Taxonomy of Personal Engagement' (Morgan and Saxton, 1987: 21–30).

HOW CAN A TEACHER READ THE LEVELS OF ENGAGEMENT IN HER STUDENTS?

Despite what educationalists, psychologists and the *Encyclopaedia Britannica* have told us, we believe, from our experience and observation, that it is possible to recognize the signs of emotional engagement; that those signs do point to degrees of involvement; and that what is gathered from a reading of those signs can inform the teacher so that she can adjust her teaching to the state of her students' engagement.

Interest

You, as a sensitive teacher, will recognize that there are different levels of student involvement in what you are teaching. Some of your students will be simply not interested, perhaps because what you are offering seems irrelevant or because some private agenda inhibits them from becoming interested. Their lack of interest may be evidenced by:

- aggressive disinterest (yawning, talking to a neighbour, reading a book etc.) or
- passive disinterest (more difficult to detect because students often take on 'the shape of interest' but you can see there is 'nothing behind the eyes').

Some will be interested because:

- they like the topic;
- you are an interesting teacher, even though the topic isn't;
- they want to learn;
- they like you and they are prepared to give you a chance.

Student interest may be evidenced by a willingness:

- to make and maintain eye contact;
- to give verbal and non-verbal responses in a supportive, congruent and appropriate manner.

In other words: Are they watching?
Are they listening?
Are they responding?

Engaging

Then there are those who are interested enough to 'go along with' whatever you want them to do: perform a task, contribute to a discussion, listen actively and so on. Their engagement is evidenced by their willingness:

- to participate;
- to follow instructions;
- to follow the rules of the classroom;
- to work independently of the teacher, either by themselves or with others.

Students who are engaging with the work generate a positive atmosphere of achieving. This is the atmosphere for which Principals and Head Teachers are always looking when they bring visitors around the school!

Committing

Other students are really 'in gear'. They are prepared to accept responsibility for their work by finding and maintaining a focus for themselves and by generating their own ideas, attitudes and points of view about the material. You can see this by:

- their absorption in the work (they are often reluctant to move on to new work within the lesson or to abandon it when the bell rings to end the lesson);
- their ability to control and manipulate the material for themselves;
- the emergence of their creative ideas;
- their confidence to challenge the direction of the work.

Students who are committing are demonstrating a considerable amount of personal investment in the work which makes it possible for the next level to come into play.

Internalizing

There is nothing easier to recognize, nor more difficult to describe in behavioural terms, than what happens to those students for whom 'the lights are going on'. This level of engagement, described by Bruner (1986), Vygotsky (1986) and others as 'internalization' is crucial to long-term understanding. If it is not reached the student will be engaged only in short-term learning and what appears to be 'understanding' will melt away when the need for it is no longer there. For example, knowledge 'crammed' for a test or examination is forgotten before the holidays have scarcely begun.

In Internalizing the drive to understand is fuelled by feelings of excitement, concentration, perplexity and, often, anxiety. This is followed by feelings of relief, satisfaction and calm: the storm has been 'weathered'; the mind has moved from confusion to order – from a state of unrelated pieces to a connected whole. The experience is rather like finding the piece of a 'jigsaw' that suddenly reveals a section of the puzzle. You may see this in students as their facial expressions change from concentration to relief or their posture changes from tension to relaxation. Sometimes the 'merging' appears to be instantaneous: a 'revelation'; the 'light bulb goes on' or, as it has been described by a student, 'Its a sort of gut-thunk!' On the other hand, it may be that you can see 'the wheels slowly turning' until that flash of understanding, 'Just a moment, everyone. I think I've got it! ...(pause)... Right! Now, I know it!' Here it appears that the student feels he knows but he has to wait for a little while for the intellect to 'catch up'.

Other students intuitively recognize that what they are learning has meaning for them but it often takes much longer for the personal, empathetic relationship with the new knowledge to develop. It is not until they attempt to express that meaning (Interpreting) and to test it out (Evaluating) that they realize that they do know what they now know.

Whether it happens quickly or slowly, the student is seeing the relationship between what he is thinking and feeling and doing *now* with what he already knows, feels and has experienced. The result of making these connections is a new realization, a different way of understanding. It is this which establishes for him a sense of control over what he is learning. Both teacher and students 'will have no difficulty in knowing that a shift in understanding has taken place. Call it a "moment of truth", an "aesthetic experience" or "peak experiencing"' as Maslow (1968: 79) does, we do not need a 'check list of behavioural evidence to verify that internalization has occurred' (Morgan and Saxton, 1987: 25).

Interpreting

Once students have begun to make connections between their own experience and the material they are studying, they can and need to move into another level of engagement. You will recognize those students as the ones who are willing to talk about the work because:

• they are anxious to hear what others think and feel and are prepared to defend their points of view and to share their own feelings and opinions;

- they are willing to reconsider their responses and adapt their conclusions in the light of new information and ideas;
- they have the confidence to submit their feelings and ideas for analysis and consideration by others;
- they are anxious to make predictions and to consider the implications of their thinking;
- they are gripped by the possibilities of their new understanding and are anxious to make it concrete in some way: by writing, graphics, debate or by applying their conclusions to other situations and so on.

It is worth noting that some students who have undergone a very deep internalizing experience will not want to share their thoughts and feelings right away, and sometimes not for a long time. A sensitive teacher will respect this need for privacy and distance.

Evaluating

The final level of engagement is revealed when students want to test their new understanding on someone who has not been involved in the process. They need to confirm it by trying it out in some more formal way in a more public forum:

- by talking at home about what they understand (this is often misconstrued by parents as 'being preached at!');
- by discussing it with their peers in school but outside the classroom;
- by introducing the ideas in another class (sometimes resented by the other teacher); or
- by writing an article for the school paper, and so on.

THE TAXONOMY AND OWNERSHIP

A taxonomy is a way of classifying and is cumulative: the next level always builds upon the one before. Because what is happening in a lesson depends upon the manner in which you offer the material and also upon your students' past experiences and knowledge, students will not necessarily all engage at the same level at the same time and they may shift back and forth through the levels during the lesson. However, students must always move through the sequence if they are to capture the full significance of the work for *them*. Sequential progression is necessary to the deepening of their engagement with, and their eventual ownership of, the material. It is this 'process of ownership' (Malczewski, 1990: 204–6, see also Woods, 1987: 125) that encourages students to find fresh perspectives and to gain understanding about the issues and materials which are being explored. 'True ownership occurs when we see ourselves in the thing owned and recognize that it is an integral part of us' (Saxton and Verriour, 1988). This sense of owning, of being in control of their learning, gives students a feeling of increasing satisfaction as they see that what began as the teacher's is becoming their own; as they move from 'seeing themselves as people to whom things happen to seeing themselves as people who can make things happen' (Schaffner, 1983: 40).

Effective teaching requires more than knowing what you are going to teach, why you are teaching it and to whom you are teaching it. It is recognizing that all students bring their feelings, as well as their minds and bodies, into the classroom. Understanding how you can engage and capitalize on this 'internal state' of needs, preferences, anxieties, curiosity and excitement will be the dynamic which transforms the classroom into a place where learning is recognized by the students as something to be valued for itself rather than as a means to someone else's evaluation.

HOW DOES THE TAXONOMY FIT INTO QUESTIONING?

Here is an exercise: the class is beginning the study of 'earthworms' as part of a unit in Environmental Studies. If you were a student knowing little or nothing about earthworms, which questions would have the greatest potential to engage your interest?

1 How is the earthworm valuable to man?
2 Charles Darwin brought our attention to the value of the earthworm as a preserver of our heritage. I wonder what he meant?
3 What do you use at the end of your hook when you go fishing?
4 Which would you rather take for a headache: an aspirin or an earthworm?

Why did you choose that particular question?

If you chose 1, it might be because you thought you knew the answer. On the other hand, you might not choose it because it's a stupid question – isn't that what you suspect the unit will be about?

If you chose 2, it might be that you wanted to find out the relationship between the lowly earthworm and the Parthenon – a genuine curiosity. On the other hand, you might not choose it because you don't think 'Charles Darwin' sounds very interesting.

If you chose 3, it might be because you learned how to worm a hook this summer and want to share your accomplishment. On the other hand, you didn't choose it because you know the answer (doesn't everyone?) and you can't see where the question is going.

If you chose 4, it might be because you had a visceral reaction and are attracted by the macabre. On the other hand, you might not choose it because this book, so far, has given you a headache and the last thing you want to do is to take two worms with a glass of water!

There are an infinite number of reasons why a question attracts students. Questions interest them because there is something in them which connects with what is being presented or offered. John Holt (1982: 163) writes that learning happens when it becomes important to ask: 'What's that, what's it for, how do you work it?' There can certainly be no change in understanding unless the question holds the possibility of an answer with personal meaning for the student. The more you know about students' backgrounds, interests and experiences, the greater chance you have of choosing a question that holds that possibility.

Let's take another example

You and your English Literature students have just seen a production of Arthur Miller's *The Crucible*. Which of the following questions would have the greatest potential for engaging their interest in discussion?

1 How did the production reflect the atmosphere of the period?
2 What part of the play did you like best? Why?
3 There are many television shows and movies about demonic possession, how do they compare with *The Crucible*?
4 From watching the play, what new insights do you have into the failure of the marriage between John and Elizabeth?

Now, look at all four questions and, as we did with the 'earthworms' exercise, decide why your students might, or might not, be caught by a particular question. To do this it is not necessary for you to know the play but only to be able to see clearly what each question has to offer in terms of what you know about the students you teach.

How do I use the taxonomy to help me frame my questions?

When we use the taxonomy as a guide for inviting and sustaining students' engagement with the material, we ask ourselves the following:

● What questions shall I ask which will attract their attention? *[Interest]*
● What questions shall I ask which will draw them into active involvement, where their ideas become an important part of the process? *[Engaging]*
● What questions shall I ask which will invite them to take on responsibility for the inquiry? *[Committing]*
● What questions shall I ask which will create an environment in which they will have opportunities to reflect upon their personal thoughts,

feelings, attitudes, points of view, experiences and values in relation to the material of the lesson? *[Internalizing]*

● What questions shall I ask which will invite them to express their understanding of the relationship between their subjective world, the world of their peers and the world of the subject matter. What opportunities shall I provide which will enable them to formulate new questions which arise from their new understanding? *[Interpreting]*

● What questions shall I ask which will provide them with opportunities to test their new thinking in different media? *[Evaluating]*

We can see from the 'Taxonomy of Personal Engagement' that a successful lesson depends upon a teacher's awareness of the levels of student engagement, her responses to what she hears and senses as she observes the students working with their peers, the material and herself. The taxomony functions in three ways:

1 It is the means by which a teacher generates and maintains student involvement in learning.
2 It is the agent through which the objective world of the material is brought into a relationship and made congruent with the subjective world of the student.
3 It is the process through which students themselves come to control and to own their learning.

What are the implications for the teacher?

● You will have to learn to see the emotional climate of the classroom as an important indication of the quality of the learning.

● You must understand that implicit within the 'Taxonomy of Personal Engagement' is the notion of transfer or 'handover'. Edwards and Mercer (1987: 23) call this 'the action which signifies the end of the need for a teacher or tutor,' as 'students come to take control of the process for themselves.'

You will find that working with the emotional climate of the classroom rather than ignoring or trying to work against it, will remove you from an adversarial position and put you in a partnership with your students. As they begin to control how they are learning, you, in turn, have to spend less time in the roles of disciplinarian and classroom manager. You will be free to take on other teaching stances which can offer you, as well as your students, rich opportunities for learning.

Let us now look at a lesson . . . .

Chapter 4

The example lesson: 'Snow White'

We have chosen this lesson because the material with which the teacher is working should be familiar to you, freeing you from a concern with the content, to examine the educational context. We point out the two taxonomies and you will see how 'Bloom's taxonomy' operates non-sequentially. We also point out some of the ways in which the teacher gives her students opportunities to 'invest' themselves in the material and to control the course of the exploration.[1]

CLASS DESCRIPTION

Subject: Language Arts/Art
Class: Grade 4 (10 years old)
Type: 30 students, 16 boys, 14 girls (mixed ethnic backgrounds)
Class shows: 1. Poor command of English.
                2. Reluctance to speak and to read.
                3. Restless behaviour (just able to sit still and listen).
                4. Low self-esteem.
Teacher's objectives: To provide the kind of opportunity which will encourage students to listen; to use language; to succeed; to express their feelings through other media (writing and art).

THE PLAN

Number of lessons: 2 or 3   Time: 1 hour
                                             (afternoons)

Step outline:
1. Explain what we are going to do:
    ● Show picture of castle?
Possible question (PQ)1: What kinds of people might live in a building like this?

KNOWING The teacher is promoting:	ENGAGEMENT The teacher is promoting:	CONTROLLING/OWNING The teacher is inviting:

(1) Applying	Interest	Students' input

- Connect to 'soaps' on TV?

PQ2: Stories of long ago had the same kind of violence and magic as you see on TV. Can we all go back to those dark and dangerous times?

(2) Recalling	Engaging	Students' agreement

2 Let them give suggestions for the names of a girl and a boy.
3 Tell them I will be someone in the story (demonstrate?)
4 Tell story of 'Snow White' up to Huntsman's dilemma, then try going into role as the Huntsman. They should remember this but they may need some reminding. Hope not.

PQ3: Do you think I should obey the order of the Queen and kill the Princess? (Acknowledge the difficulty of the problem but keep the story going – no implications.)

(3) Judging	Engaging	Opportunity for control

5 Read the next bit till Queen goes to the Apothecary.

PQ4: Can you sell me some poison? How much will you sell me? (If they won't give, go back to story and say the Queen will make her own out of deadly nightshade!)

(4) Judging	Engaging	Opportunity for control

6 Tell story to the point where Queen wants to put poison in the apples.

PQ5: How would someone poison an apple? (Try for pair work here.)

(5) Recalling/Creating	Committing	Opportunity for control

7 Continue to the selling of the apples.

PQ6: Will you buy one of my lovely, red apples? (Offer to at least six or eight students.)

KNOWING The teacher is promoting:	ENGAGEMENT The teacher is promoting:	CONTROLLING/OWNING The teacher is inviting:
(6) Applying/Judging/ Recalling	Committing	Opportunity for control

8 Throw them a curve!
   PQ7: How do I get to the miners' house?

(7) Creating/Judging	Committing	Opportunity for control

9 On with the story to the end of the visit with Snow White. Get them to
   tell the story of the 'witch' and the apples – to me? to a partner?
   PQ8: What happened in the village today?

(8) Creating	Engaging	Opportunity for ownership

10 On to introduce the Prince (name they gave me).
   Task: Draw and/or write the end of the story.
   PQ9: A lot of stories end 'happily ever after'. What is the end of your story?

(9) Creating/Recalling/ Reasoning	Committing > Interpreting	Opportunity for ownership

11 Put pictures on wall (Parents' Night date?).
12 Read the end of the story.

Administration:

Check supplies, crayons, paint, water tins, paper, copy of *Life* magazine
with castles in it. Music?

THE LESSON / WHAT ACTUALLY HAPPENED

Day 1

Teacher: 'When we were in the Library yesterday, many of you chose
stories about magic and witches. Today, I'm going to tell you a story about
those things but I'm going to need your help.'

KNOWING The teacher is promoting:	ENGAGEMENT The teacher is promoting:	CONTROLLING/OWNING The teacher is inviting:

Q1: 'How did Mr Longstaffe start his story yesterday?'

(1) Recalling	Interest	Student input

R1: 'He said, 'This happened a long time ago.' (Two other similar replies) 'Good. That's the kind of help I am going to need today.'

Q2: 'Before I begin, can you give me names for a girl and a boy that are different from all the names in our class? They will be the names of the heroine and the hero, so you will need to think about this and choose carefully.'

(2) Recalling Understanding	Engaging	Opportunity for ownership

R2: After a number of suggestions, they choose 'Linda' and 'Emilio'. 'Thank you.'

Narration: 'Once upon a time, there was a little girl who lived with her father. Her mother had died when she was ten. Her father was a King and so she was a Princess. One day her father came to her and told her that he wished to marry again. When the little girl, whose name was Linda, met her step-mother-to-be, she saw she was a very beautiful woman, who seemed kind and interested in her. She was not surprised that her father, the King, was in love with the woman.

As time went on, Linda began to understand that the most important thing in her step-mother's life was not Linda, nor Linda's father, but her own beauty. The Queen, for that was what she now was, went every day to her magic mirror . . .

R3: (A student says, 'I know that story'. Teacher acknowledges with a conspiratorial smile)

. . . and asked it to tell her who was the most beautiful woman in the kingdom. And everyday the mirror replied that it was the Queen herself.

Now one day, when the Queen went to her mirror and asked it the question she asked every day, the mirror replied,

"Though you, O Queen, are very fair,
Linda is she beyond compare."

And the Queen fell into a rage and called to her Huntsman and ordered him to take Linda into the depths of the forest and kill her. The Huntsman was appalled that he should be ordered to kill Linda and all day and all night

KNOWING The teacher is promoting:	ENGAGEMENT The teacher is promoting:	CONTROLLING/OWNING The teacher is inviting:

he wrestled with his conscience. In despair, he went to his closest friend whom he loved and trusted, and said to him . . . '

> In her narration, the teacher supports the students' contributions in order to promote ownership.

(Teacher 'in role' as the Huntsman)

Q3: 'I don't know what to do. I've known Linda all her life. What do you think I should do?'

(3) Solving	Engaging	Opportunity for control

R4: She turns to a student who looks at her wide-eyed.

Q4: 'Do you think I should obey the order of the Queen and kill Linda?'

(4) Judging	Engaging	Opportunity for control

R5: 'I don't know.'

Q5: 'It is difficult, isn't it?'

(5) Judging	Engaging	——

She turns to three other students, repeating Question 4, adding 'What should I do?'

(4a) Judging	Engaging	Opportunity for control

R6: 'You should kill her.'

'Then I would be obeying the Queen's orders.'

R7: 'I don't think you should.'

Narration: 'Some of my friends are telling me "yes" and some are telling me "no". I will use their advice to make up my own mind.'

'The Huntsman thought long and hard but in the end he could not kill Linda. He took her into the dark forest and told her what the Queen had

KNOWING The teacher is promoting:	ENGAGEMENT The teacher is promoting:	CONTROLLING/OWNING The teacher is inviting:

wanted him to do and then, leaving her with a little food, he ran away himself from the Queen's vengeance.

When the Queen went to her mirror the next day, she was expecting a very different answer from the one she received:

"Though you, O Queen, are very fair,
Linda is she beyond compare."

And the Queen fell into a rage. She knew that the Huntsman had failed her and now she must do the wicked deed herself. She went to the Apothecary, the one who makes medicines, and said to him . . . '

Q6 (Teacher in role as the Queen): 'Do you know who I am?' (She approaches a student)

(6) Recalling	Interest	——

R8: 'No.'
Q7: 'I am the Queen. Do you know why I am here?'

(7) Recalling	Interest	——

R9: 'No.'
Q8: 'I am here to buy poison. Will you sell me some?'

(8) Understanding/Judging	Engaging	——

R10: 'No.'
'Thank you. I will now go and ask the apothecary down the road.' (She tries another student)
Q9: 'Do you know who I am?'

(9) Recalling	Interest>Engaging	——

R11: 'You're the Queen.'
Q10: 'Do you know why I am here?'

(10) Recalling	Interest>Engaging	——

KNOWING The teacher is promoting:	ENGAGEMENT The teacher is promoting:	CONTROLLING/OWNING The teacher is inviting:

R12: 'You want to buy some poison.'
Q11: 'Will you sell me some?'

(11) Understanding/ Judging	Engaging	Opportunity for control

R13: 'How much do you want?' (He gives her some)
'Thank you.' She moves to the next student who tells her before she says anything...
R14: 'My mother keeps rat poison in the cupboard. I'm not allowed there.'
'That poison must be very strong. I'm sorry you can't give me any.' She turns to the next student.
Q12: 'Do you have any poison that will kill very big rats?'

(12) Recalling/ Understanding/ Reasoning	Engaging> Committing	Opportunity for control

R15: 'How much do you need?'
Q13: 'How much do you think I should have?'

(13) Recalling/Judging	Committing	Opportunity for control

R16: 'This much.' (Student hands her something)
She turns to three more students and asks them Q12 and Q13.
R17... All of them give her some poison.
Narration: 'When the Queen felt that she had enough poison, she went down the stone steps where the apples are stored. She filled two baskets to the top with beautiful, red apples – the best that she could find. She poured all the poisons she had collected into her large black kettle and, while it was cooking, she sat down to think how she would put the poison into the apples so that no one would know.'

The teacher confirms contributions, providing opportunities for ownership.

KNOWING The teacher is promoting:	ENGAGEMENT The teacher is promoting:	CONTROLLING/OWNING The teacher is inviting:

Q14: 'How would she have done that?'

(14) Solving	Engaging	Opportunity for control

R18: No reply.
Q15: 'How could someone poison an apple so that no one would know the poison was there? Just talk to the person next to you.'

(15) Recalling/Solving	Interest> Engaging	Opportunity for control

R19: Most students had difficulty in working with a partner, not because they weren't interested but because they had difficulty in listening to the other's suggestions. The teacher collects their ideas which included: a needle, dipping the apple in the poison, a laser, making an apple pie, making a spell....

Narration: 'Soon she had a basketful of poisoned apples which looked just like the basket of good apples. No one could tell the difference. The Queen sent out her spies all over the land and it soon became clear to her that there was only one place that Linda could be. In the depths of the dark forest, in a glade, there was a little cabin in which the King's gold miners lived. It was rumoured that they were harbouring a young woman who was working as their housekeeper. Although no one had ever seen her, rumour had it that she was gentle, kind, and loving – some said that they had heard that she was indeed the daughter of the King, whom no one had seen for many months.

And so the Queen disguised herself as an itinerant merchant – a purveyor of small goods: needles, threads and other useful household items – and she took upon herself the clothing and appearance of an old woman. She picked up both baskets of apples and walked to the village at the edge of the wood. She came to the first house and knocked on the door.'

The teacher takes back control to keep the story 'on track'.

Q16: 'Would you like, Sir, to buy one of my beautiful, red, rosy apples?'

KNOWING The teacher is promoting:	ENGAGEMENT The teacher is promoting:	CONTROLLING/OWNING The teacher is inviting:
(16) Judging	Engaging> Committing	Opportunity for control

R20: 'No, thank you.' She turns to another student, who without being asked, says,

R21: 'No, thank you. We don't like apples.' She turns to another student who, again without being asked, says,

R22: (pointing to the 'good' apples) 'I'll have an apple from that basket.' She continues the business, with most children accepting an apple from the 'good' basket. She turns to the group.

Q17: 'Can anyone tell me how to get to the house where the gold miners live? I know they like apples!'

(17) Judging	Committing	Opportunity for control

R23: 'They live in the woods.'
R24: (quickly) 'They don't live there any more!'
Q18: 'Are you sure?'

(18) Reasoning/Creating	Committing	Opportunity for control

R25: They begin to talk amongst themselves – a mix of directions, misdirections and should they or should they not tell her anything.

Narration: 'So the Queen found the path into the woods and came to the little house and knocked upon the door. And when Linda saw the enchanted apple, she bought the whole basket so that she could make a pie for her friends, the goldminers. But she could not resist taking a bite from the apple and no sooner did she taste the apple than she fell down upon the ground and was still.

The miners, returning home from work passed through the village and heard the villagers talking about the visit of the apple seller.'

The teacher confirms students' ideas.

Q19: 'What stories did the villagers tell the miners?'

KNOWING The teacher is promoting:	ENGAGEMENT The teacher is promoting:	CONTROLLING/OWNING The teacher is inviting:

(19) Recalling/Creating	Committing	Opportunity for ownership

R26: 'They said an old woman came selling apples.'
R27: 'And she wanted to know the way to your house!'
Q20: 'Had anyone ever seen her before?'

(20) Recalling/Creating	Committing	Opportunity for control

R28: A generous burst of information, including the fact that the old woman looked a lot like the Queen!

Narration: 'When they heard that, the miners hurried home only to find what they had feared. They saw Linda lying on the floor. They listened for her heartbeat but it was still; they checked to see if she was breathing but nothing stirred. They laid her in a glass coffin and carried it to the woods.

And it came to pass that a King's son, whose name was Prince Emilio, was visiting from a faraway land and he heard the story of the beautiful lady who lay in the woods.'

The teacher uses information as emotional 'sub-text' for the narrative.

Q21: 'What do you think will happen now?'

(21) Creating	Internalizing> Interpreting	Opportunity for control

Q22: 'How do you want the story to end?'

(22) Creating	Interpreting	Opportunity for control

Instruction: 'Close your eyes or look down at your desk to help you think to yourself how you want the story to end' (Quiet for slightly more than a minute.)

'Draw a picture which will show me what you think happened.'

KNOWING The teacher is promoting:	ENGAGEMENT The teacher is promoting:	CONTROLLING/OWNING The teacher is inviting:

Q23: 'I wonder where you would put yourself in your picture?'

(23) Creating/Judging	Interpreting	Opportunity for control

R29: The remaining class time was spent in working in crayon-resist. Much of the art was quite detailed and many of the students added writing to their pictures. The teacher noted that the students were much more interested in the content of each others' work than formerly. Although there was much moving about, it was mainly purposeful and non-aggressive.

Day 2

In the morning, the teacher and students arrange the pictures on the wall.

The 'picture gallery': All categories of both taxonomies are in play during this time as the students talk amongst themselves about the story, their parts in it, their pictures and how these should be placed and why.

Towards the end of the discussion, rearranging, peer questioning and admiring, one of the students asks the teacher,
    Q24: (Student): 'I wonder what happened to "her" Dad – he just sort of disappeared, didn't he?'

(24) (Student Question) Solving	Interpreting	Demonstrating ownership

R30: (Teacher): 'I wonder, too.'
They all look at the pictures thoughtfully.
    Q25: 'Shall I read you the rest of the story of Linda this afternoon?'

(25) Judging	Evaluating	Teacher hands over control

R31: 'Why?'
'I thought you might like to hear someone else's ending to the story.'
By their lack of enthusiasm, the teacher recognizes that the students are

satisfied with their own work. She tells them, 'I'll leave the story on the window shelf. Here are two other versions of the same story, as well, for you to look at and compare with your own.'

SUMMARY

The teacher, through her questions, has provided a lesson which, because of her use of a story, has potential for capturing interest. She uses her story-telling techniques to make it easier for her students to listen and to maintain their interest.

By her use of role (for herself and her students) she gives them opportunities for using language spontaneously in a variety of ways in a non-pressured experience. Roles support the students' involvement with the material as well as giving them a strong measure of control over the teacher (e.g. as Queen). Role also provides opportunities for this restless class to have reasons for moving about.

In this lesson we see the teacher accepting and responding to her students' levels of engagement but also offering opportunities for deepening involvement. You will note that the kinds of thinking demanded of her students through questions are not tied to the sequential imperative of the taxonomy of 'knowing'. There is, however, a high degree of complex thinking from these students, as evidenced by their responses.

In providing a conclusion in which they complete the story in their own way, the teacher allows her students individually and privately to take control of the story and to have the satisfaction of interpreting an ending which has personal meaning for them. Despite her hope to have them compare their endings to that of the orginal fairy tale, she is prepared, in asking Question 25, to hand over the ownership of the material to her students and they are willing to take it. The 'picture gallery' activity the next day enables them, through cooperative action and discussion, to see their work both as an individual and as a collective expression of response to the story.

When we examine the questions that the teacher asks during these two lessons, we see questions which tap into the students' backgrounds and experiences; questions which invite the students to contribute their own ideas and directions; which promote responses that come from the 'heart' as well as the 'head' and which let the students, collectively, take over the story. What we don't see here are many students engaged in question-asking although there is quite a lot of peer questioning during the 'talk' times. Question-asking, for these students, is inhibited both by their lack of skill with language and with their cultural perceptions of who has the 'right' to ask the questions. Despite this, you can see that the teacher's questions do not exist in isolation – nor do her students' answers.

Questions have a wider purpose than simply as a means to a reply. They enable students to bring their own thoughts and feelings into expression either through the answer or through their own questions. Teachers and students must learn to see questions not as hurdles which must be got over in order to prove intelligence but as expressions of genuine interest that demand careful listening and thoughtful consideration. When this is understood, classroom discourse is vigorous and productive as questions and answers are woven together in the process of inquiry. The warp that holds the pattern of the discourse is made up of thought and feeling and it is teachers' attention to providing diversity in ways of thinking, and opportunities for engaging through many levels, that will enable their students to 'own' their learning.

ANY QUESTIONS?

'You bet I have! I understand that I have to pay attention to feeling as well as to thinking and I can see that questions shouldn't be tied to 'Bloom's taxonomy' but I hope you have something to help me make better questions. After all this theory, I need a little *practical* assistance.'

Relax! That's what the next section is all about.

Part II

What kind of question?

Chapter 5

A classification of questions

Questions, like students, have an active role to play in the learning process. Whereas other classifications of questioning identify their categories by type – for example, factual, conceptual, contextual, we offer one that identifies a general *intention* for each category. Rather than asking ourselves 'What *type* of questions should I ask?', we, and our students, find it more practical to ask ourselves 'What do I want this question to *do*?'.

The classification has three broad categories and each category has a specific intention. We will outline these first and then go on to provide a series of sources with examples.

A CLASSIFICATION OF QUESTIONS BY GENERAL FUNCTION[1]

Category A: Questions which elicit information: These are the questions which draw out what is already known in terms of both information and experience and which establish the appropriate procedures for the conduct of the work.

Category B: Questions which shape understanding: These are questions which help teachers and students fill in what lies between the facts and sort out, express and elaborate how they are thinking and feeling about the material.

Category C: Questions which press for reflection: These are the questions which demand intellectual and emotional commitment by challenging the individual to think critically and creatively.

The three categories reflect these principles:

- Students have the right to be participators in their education and must be offered the means by which they can share responsibility for their learning.
- The collective nature of the classroom must be acknowledged. Students come to understand things by building joint frames of reference which enable them to participate in learning as a social and cultural process – which is not 'merely one of individual discovery but one of sharing,

comparing, contrasting and arguing one's perspective against those of others' (Edwards and Mercer, 1987: 164).

- Every individual needs and has the right to be provoked into a consideration of his ideas at the deepest levels of thought and feeling and he must be given time for reflection. As Bruner (1986: 127) puts it, 'Much of the process of education consists of being able to distance oneself in some way from what one knows by being able to reflect on one's knowledge.'

The functions of these categories are all equally important in the learning process, demanding different kinds of thinking. But research shows that most questions asked in classrooms, whether by teachers or students, fall into Category A. The questions which shape understanding and demand reflection are those which relate most closely to the levels of internalizing and interpreting in the Taxonomy of Personal Engagement. In other words, if you want your students to think about what they are learning in such a way that learning becomes a part of their view of themselves and of their world, you will have to ask questions which help them to articulate meaning and cause them to think about the meaning that is being made.

Within every category there are a range of questions, each one of which serves a particular function. On the following pages we example these in order to show you the limitless possibilities of questions to mediate content, process and investment.

CATEGORY A: GENERAL FUNCTION: eliciting information

Particular functions:

1. Questions that establish the 'rules of the game '

'What do we need to remember so we don't get in the way of the work?'
Function: A means of setting rules of behaviour or reminding students of rules they have set previously.

'Can we manage without raising hands?'
Function: To develop discussion skills by giving the students the responsibility for the ordering of the answers.

'What rules shall we make about late-comers?'
Function: To guarantee the smooth operation of the class with minimum intrusion.

'Have you been listening?'
'Can everyone see?'
'Did anyone have trouble hearing Ted?'
'Can everyone hear?'

Function: To insure a good working atmosphere where individuals monitor the situation for themselves.

2. Questions that establish procedure

'Which order shall we go in?'
'Would it help if you talked this over with someone else?'
'How shall we re-form the groups?'
'Do you want to do this, or that?'
'Do we need to make a note of this?'
Function: To help students to consider the most productive ways for work.

'How are we going to do that?'
'Where should we do that?'
'How much time do you need?'
'How much *more* time do you need?'
'How can we do that more efficiently?'
Function: To encourage students to develop organization of time and space or method of work.

'Do we know enough to go on?'
'Have we enough material on which to base our conclusions?'
'What do we need to know now?'
'Can you manage on your own?'
Function: To establish students' engagement in the material.

'Where can we find that information?'
'Who will be able to give us that information?'
Function: To stimulate research.

3. Questions which establish or help to control group discipline

'What size group will work best for you?'
'How will you arrange yourselves in the group?'
'Who will be responsible for keeping notes?'
'Who in the group has a watch?'
'How shall we arrange the desks?'
Function: To help students work efficiently in groups independent of the teacher.

4. Questions which unify the class

'Are we all agreed that . . .?'
'Are we ready to go on?'

'Has anyone anything to add?'
'Will you accept that for the moment?'
Function: To ensure that we can move along together.

5. Questions which focus on recall of facts

'What is the formula?'
'What were the terms of the will?'
'Could you summarize the main points so far?'
'What do we now know?'
Function: To share facts in order to establish a firm foundation for further work.

6. Questions which supply information and/or suggest implications

'With all the extra time it will require, are you still prepared to undertake the art display?'
'When the Principal asks you to explain the arrangements, what will you tell him?'
Function: To prepare students to deal with a possible challenge or to focus on the parameters of response.

7. Questions which reveal experience

'What sorts of ideas do you have when you hear the phrase "rights of the individual"?'
'What kinds of experiences lead people to behave in that way?'
Function: To discover what personal luggage students are bringing with them to the content of the lesson.

The examples above do not require a context because they deal with the operation of the lesson, whatever the material. In order to understand the following categories we have selected a number of sources which we hope will not only clarify the thrust of the questions but also be of interest to you. We have italicized the words and phrases which can be transferred to other contexts.

CATEGORY B: GENERAL FUNCTION: shaping understanding

Particular functions:

1. Questions which focus on making connections

Source:

'When Canada was a very young country, people had little means of sending messages. Very rich people living in Quebec or Montreal sent private messengers from one place or the other to carry packets of letters to their friends. Sometimes people were lucky enough to persuade the Government courier to carry letters for them and, in spring when the hunters returned to Three Rivers, Montreal or Quebec, they also distributed news. Indeed, their homecoming was an event of great importance, if for no other reason than that they could give news of the settlers whom they had seen along the way, and could deliver messages entrusted to them.'

(Moore and McEwen, 1936: 76)

- '*What connections are there between* this and the kind of thing which happens in our own lives?'
- '*How would it change* your lives if you were in a similar situation where communication was so apparently limited?'
- '*I wonder if people have always had and will always have* the same reactions as the settlers when communication is re-established?'
- '*What has this* source *to do with* the fact that the art of letter-writing is dying out?'
- '*By what means* could the outposts communicate with the populated centres in an emergency?'

Function: To require students to use what they know and apply it to the material at hand; to bring students today into a relationship with the past and/or the future.

2. Questions which press students to rethink or restate by being more accurate and specific

Source:

' . . . I believe that the whole state of higher education is going to get worse. If my subject was flourishing and the universities were being treated in a more civilized way, it would be different . . . '

(Blackburn, 1988)

- '*What do you mean by* "civilized"?'
- '*How do you perceive* "it *would be* different?"'
- '*Can you put that in a way that* the general public would understand?'

Function: To press for intellectual clarity when the meaning is veiled.

or

Source:
'Everyone HATES Physics!'
(A student, any day, any time, any year . . .)

- 'What is it about your Physics that makes you feel so strongly?'
- 'Is it just Physics that worries you?'
- 'What specific situation triggered this?'

Function: To press for intellectual clarity when emotion clouds the meaning.

3. Questions which help promote expression of attitudes, biases and points of view

Source:
'The Temagami wilderness controversy is smouldering like fire creeping through the undergrowth. After six months of increasing smoke, many of those involved warn that the confrontation over the Northern Ontario forest will erupt into an all-out blaze. The main question is not when it will start but who will start it.

Will it be the natives of the Teme-Augama Anishnabal (Deep Water People) who have vowed to continue their six-month blockade of access to a forest they say includes sacred grounds that are part of a larger, unresolved land claim?

Will it be the environmentalists, who are suing the province to protect a wilderness buffer around Lady Evelyn Smoothwater provincial park? The area is one of 76 threatened sites on a global register kept by the International Union for Conservation of Nature and Natural Resources, the world's largest alliance of conservation groups. Or will it be the loggers and town business leaders who have long claimed that the timber in the disputed area is vital to their economic survival?

The Temagami issue has often been painted as a north versus south struggle, pitting northern jobs and incomes against southern canoeists and tree worshippers. But wilderness outfitters also want the area saved, noting that about one-third of the Temagami economy depends on tourism untainted by the ravages of logging. . . . There are as many people in this area saying: "Save the wilderness" as there are saying: "Let them cut." '
(Kathleen Kenna, 1988)

- 'Who would want to be in the logging industry today?'
- 'Would you rather preserve the environment and be unemployed or preserve your job and let nature look after itself . . . after all . . .?'
- 'Where do you stand on this?'
- 'As a citizen and taxpayer, what are your concerns?'

- *'If it were* happening in your own backyard, *would you feel differently?'*
- *'Is it possible* to live in an area of conflict and belong to no side?'
- *'How will* the inhabitants' perceptions of their world *be changed* by this controversy?'

Function: To help develop attitudes to the area of study; to present opportunities for seeing material from a variety of viewpoints and to respect the attitudes and points of view of others; to become aware of the emotional power that is attached to ideas.

4. Questions which demand inference and interpretation

Source:

'Computers are a recent addition to the learning environment. They are useful in providing extensions of and support for science learning. They also help overcome restrictions of cost, time, accessibility and safety through simulations of expensive, time-consuming and dangerous activities. Computers should not, however, be regarded as a primary means of delivering science education or as a replacement for the direct investigation of natural and physical phenomena.'

(Ontario Ministry of Education, 1988)

- *'How would you explain* to the people who hold the purse strings, that computers are an important and necessary adjunct to the science curriculum?'
- *'What might be implied by* the sentence, "Computers should not ... be regarded as a primary means of delivering science education?" '
- *'How will* the Arts teachers perceive this expenditure?'

Function: To require students to consider, justify and/or explain textual statements, situations or conclusions.

5. Questions which focus on meanings that lie behind the actual content

Source:

'A married couple in a Western state ... ran a house of prostitution, using three older women whom they treated abominably. Then one Fourth of July they suddenly decided to give the 'girls' a vacation, all expenses paid. Drove them to Yellowstone Park, treated them to a great time, and as they drove home to put the girls back to work, they said "Girls, we appreciate your help,"and the girls said "Thanks".

Well, the Utah authorities arrested the couple for violating the Mann Act, bringing the women back across the state line for immoral purposes. Caught dead to rights, no contest, big fine and long prison sentences for the culprits ... some judge wrote a most moving decision. Said the facts in the case were irrefutable, the Mann Act had been transgressed, a crime had been committed, and the punishment was not unreasonable. But, he added, sometimes the law hands down a judgement which offends the rule of common sense ... the state could properly have arrested the couple at any time during the past dozen years for wrong that they were committing, but they waited until the pair was doing the right thing... bringing their girls back from a paid holiday. The sense of propriety on which society must rely had been offended. Case reversed. Couple set free.'

(Michener, 1987: 173)

- *'What is this* case really *about?'*
- *'What have we discovered about* judges and the law?'
- *'What place has* a 'sense of propriety' in judgements which are, or should be, based on precedent?'
- *'Why do you think* the proprietors suddenly decided to give the 'girls' a vacation?'

Function: To probe for meanings which are essential to the understanding of the material.

CATEGORY C: GENERAL FUNCTION: pressing for reflection

Particular functions:

1. Questions which develop supposition or hypothesis

Source:
    'MAN BITES DOG!'

(Newspaper headline)

- *'I wonder what* drove the man to bite the dog?'
- *'I wonder if* his wife will have to have him put down?'
- *'If* the dog was the main course, *what will* the man have for dessert?'
- *'Suppose* the man is discovered to be a veterinarian – *what then?'*
- *'What might* the neighbours be saying?'

Function: To provide students with opportunities to think creatively about the facts. In hypothesis/supposition the fact is a starting point and the questioner and responder may need to break the laws of logic.

2. Questions which focus on personal feelings

Source:
    'He saw clearly ... how much it all meant to him, and the special value of some such anchorage in one's existence. He did not at all want to abandon the new life and its splendid spaces ... and creep home and stay there. The ... world was all too strong, it called to him still ... and he knew he must return to the larger stage. But it was good to think he

had this place to come back to, this place which was all his own, these
things which were so glad to see him again and could always be counted
upon for the same simple welcome.'

(Grahame, 1908: 124)

- '*Why is it that* you sometimes feel homesick even when you are at home?'
- '*What was in your mind* as you read this passage?'
- '*Is there* any place to which you would never return – *why*?'
- '*What might be your concerns* as you prepare to move on to a "new stage"
  of your life?'

Function: To give practice in the expression and sharing of personal feelings.

3. Questions which focus on future action/projection

Source:
'"Kill Ra: eat inside his head,
    see with his inside eye."
A cloud covers the moon: I nod my head
We to sleep again: she smiling.
At light, Ra and I to shore
    looking for broken branches waves sometides leave us.
I say, "go this way." He say, "No, that way."
Again he find, I nothing.
With stick Ra found, I kill him.
With pebble on beach, break his skull open,
Eat his soft eye.
I walk back slowly,
Now Ra faster than me.
I see picture of his woman saying why? why?
Now Ra's inner tongue tells me to say:
    "The waves took him."
My woman smiles. I sit in the sun.
Now with Ra's eye inside of me I see:
Night darker than darkness,
    darkness she cannot see.'

(Ronald Duncan, undated)[2]

- '*What might happen when* he next searches for food?'
- '*How* may the last line *affect* his woman?'
- '*What are the consequences* for the three who are left?'
- '*Do* words like "salvation" and "punishment" *have*
  any meaning* in a poem such as this?'

Function: To look at implications of actions through conjecture; to
experience cause and effect; to deal with 'what is' as the basis for conjecture.

4. Questions which develop critical assessment/value judgements

Source:

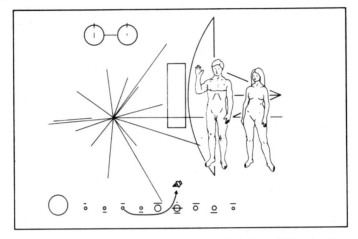

Figure 1   The 6- by 9-inch plaque carried aboard Pioneer 10

IS ANYBODY OUT THERE?

For years astronomers have searched for evidence of intelligent life beyond our solar system. Since the short-lived US Project Ozma in 1960 radio telescopes have monitored hundreds of stars, though without picking up any noteworthy signals as yet. The US space probe, Pioneer 10, launched in 1972, used another approach: a plaque designed to communicate the language of science. The hydrogen atom (the most common element in the galaxy) is shown schematically at the top. The radiating lines of binary numbers below represent specific pulsars, arranged to show the position of our sun. The humans in front of the craft illustrate the kind of creatures that built it. At the bottom is our solar system, indicating which planet is ours

(Marshall, 1977: 501)

- *'How could you* design a plaque that more truly communicates life on our planet?'
- *'How can we justify* the amount of material we hurl into space?'
- *'Does it* really *matter* to you if there is life in outer space? Why? Why not?
- *'Where would you place the value of* the space programme in relation to the needs of the Third World?'

Function: To require students to look at their value systems; to find ways of balancing feelings with intellectual analysis.

A REMINDER

These categories do not represent a taxonomy; they are *non-hierarchical*. You may introduce a question from any of the categories at any time during the lesson, depending upon your objectives, focus and your students' needs – and what you want the question *to do*.

For example, as a means of attracting student interest, a teacher of Social Studies may introduce a lesson on the causes of World War II with any of the following questions:

'Is there ever a time when someone should have the right to take over another country?' (Category B)
'How did Hitler justify his annexation of Sudetanland in 1938?' (Category A)
'If you were an arms manufacturer, how would you feel about the possibility of war?' (Category C)

Equally, any of these questions would be effective at other points in the lesson because they all deal with the teacher's major focus: Why do people go to war?

Brownlie, Close and Wingren in *Reaching for Higher Thought* (1988) develop A.V. Manzo's 'ReQuest' strategy for the teaching of reading (1969) by suggesting that students share with their teacher, the responsibility for asking questions about their reading. They offer a classification of questions which they identify as 'on the line', 'between the lines' or 'beyond the lines'. These reading comprehension questions embody the same sense of *active* intention as the three categories suggested here, that is to say, 'Will this question have to do with what is already known?' ('on the line'), 'Will this question help us shape our understanding of the facts?' ('between the lines') or 'Will this question make us think about the implications of those facts?' ('beyond the line'). Some of our student teachers use the 'line' terminology as a useful 'shorthand' for classifying their questions, whatever the subject matter.

Education is a process of inquiry and questions are the chief agents by which meanings are mediated whether they are used within discussion, to promote research, as summary or reflection, to focus the intelligence of the group, to generate a collective emotional perspective, to foster shared contexts and joint understandings, to offer springboards to new knowledge, to invite student participation, to encourage talk, to present different ways of communicating, or as a means of handing over control and a device to initiate ownership.

Now let us now look at a lesson to see how the classification operates through questions both in terms of categories and of functions.

Chapter 6

The example lesson: 'Finding areas'

We have chosen this maths lesson because it is apparently one in which students would have few opportunities for making decisions about the material, the way in which the lesson is conducted, or for contributing their own ideas. On the left-hand side we describe the progress of the lesson. On the right-hand side we suggest the category (A, B or C) and describe the particular function of the question.

CLASS DESCRIPTION

Subject: Mathematics
Class: Grade 5 (11 years old)
Type: 28 students (boys)
Class shows: 1. Reluctance to sit still behind desks.
                  2. Resentment of 'routine' work.
                  3. Lively, creative behaviour when challenged.
                  4. High self-esteem, bordering on arrogance.
Teacher's objectives: To challenge students in such a way as to focus their energy on the problem through discovery for themselves; to forge a relationship between maths and their own lives.
Administration: Thirty sheets of squared paper, extra rulers and pencils, 8 pieces of string (5m in length) and 10 copies of map.
Number of lessons: 3   Time: 40 minutes (flexible)

THE LESSON

Day 1

Category and Function

Despite the fact that the students enjoy maths once they have got down to work, they tend to enter the room reluctantly.
Q1: 'Are you ready to begin?'   (A)   Unifying class

Category and Function

Q2: 'Anyone need a pencil or ruler?'	(A) Establishing rules of the game
She hands out squared paper. 'Generally, we don't do this until Grade 6 but I thought we'd have a stab at it.'	(Here the teacher is offering a challenge.)
Q3: 'Do you think you'll be able to manage?'	(A) Suggesting implications (The teacher knows they will go along but offers the challenge in order to engage their interest.)
R1: 'Sure!'	
'The topic is "areas", specifically of rectangles and, if that goes well, we shan't have any troubles with right-angled triangles.'	
Q4: 'Where do you see a rectangle in this room?'	(A) Establishing engagement
R2: (Severally) 'Doors, windows, desk tops, John's glasses, John's head . . . '	(Teacher acknowledges their testing of her by moving on quickly.)
'Take the squared paper and, in the upper left-hand corner, draw a rectangle 3 squares long and 2 squares wide.'	
Students do so.	
Q5: 'How many squares within the figure?'	(A) Recall
R3: (Severally) 'Six squares.'	
Q6: 'How many different-sized rectangles can you draw on the top half of your page?'	(This is an instruction masquerading as a question in order to add a little challenge to the task.)
Students draw.	
Q7: 'How many squares in your various rectangles?'	(A) Recall
Students count.	
Q8: 'How many of your rectangles have the same number of squares as those of your neighbour.'	(A) Recall (Sharing in order to move along together.)
Students consult.	
Q9: 'What is the relationship between the length and width and the number of squares?'	(B) Making connections

Category and Function

R4: 'The number of squares is equal to
     the length times the width.'
Q10: 'Is James right? Check it with your   (A) Moving along together
     partner.'

Teacher draws a rectangle 3cm long
and 5cm wide.
Q11: 'If you agree that James is right   (C) Developing hypothesis
     then what might be the formula
     for finding the area of this
     rectangle where A=area, L=length
     and W=width?'
R5: 'A = L x W.
     Therefore, A = 3 x 5 = 15cm.'
Q12: 'Good. But what kind of centimetres   (C) Developing supposition
     are they?'
R6: 'They are SQUARE centimetres!
Q13: 'You bet! Now. What are the areas   (A) Recall
     of a rectangle 8cm long and 3cm
     wide and a rectangle 12cm long
     and 2cm wide?'
R7: '24 sq. cm each.'
Q14: 'What does that tell you?'   (B) Making connections
R8: 'Different shapes can have the
     same areas.'

Teacher has students test this out
with a number of examples which
they make up on their own.
Q15: 'What are the measurements of   (A) Recall
     a football field?'
Q16: 'What . . . (is its area?)'   (A) Recall
R9: Students are already telling her the
answer to the question she is about to ask.
Q17: 'We have 20 minutes left. Can you,   (A) Organizing time
     in that time, find out whether the
     far field has an area large enough
     for a football field?
     Take a 5m length of string and work
     in groups of 4.'
Q18: 'Is there a watch in each group?'   (A) Establishing discipline
     'When you get back there will be

Category and Function

questions on the board for homework.'

Students rush off enthusiastically.

Homework questions on blackboard

Q19: What is the area of the far field?	(A) Recall
Q20: Could you play a game of football on that area as it now is? Why? Why not?	(B) Interpreting and inference
Q21: I own a piece of flat grassland whose area is larger than a football field.	
Why might it be unsuitable for football?	(B) Connecting, inferring, supposing

Day 2

The class opens with a vigorous
discussion about the homework
questions and the teacher moves
back into the lesson with the following
question:

Q22: 'What kinds of people need to calculate areas?'	(A) Recall
R10: 'Architects.'	
Q23: 'Why would area measurement be important to an architect?'	(B) Connecting, inferring
R11: 'My mother says that square footage is important in selling a house.'	
R12: 'And for selling land, too.'	
Q24: 'In what other ways would the area of land be important to, say, a farmer?'	(A) for some, (B) for others. Recalling, connecting, inferring
R13: 'Taxes.'	
R14: 'For the number of cows in his field.'	
Q25: (student) 'Why would he need to know that?'	(B) Making connections
R15: 'Because you can only put so many animals in a field.'	

	Category and Function
Q26: (student) 'So? What's that mean?'	(B) Making connections
There is a long silence. The teacher implies by her silence and her stance that she is prepared to wait because this is a question worth thinking about.	
Q27: 'Who would be able to tell us?'	(A) Researching
R16: 'She knows!'	
Q28: 'Yes. Do you want me to tell you?'	(A) Deciding procedure
Naturally they nod!	
'It has something to do with eating.'	
Students discuss in groups and come up with the answer: every cow has to have so much land on which to graze. 'Well done! I don't know about cows but I do know that one sheep in southern Ontario needs 1000 sq. m for maximum health.'	
Q29: 'How many sheep could we run on the far field?'	(B) Connecting
Q30: 'If we want to reseed the far field, what will we need to know?'	(C) Supposing
There is a general discussion which allows the teacher to assess whether the class is ready to move on.	

Homework

Q31: How can you find the area of a right-angled triangle which has a height of 5cm and a base of 4cm.	(B) Connecting
Q32: 'Bill. Will you find out from your uncle the amount of land required for running a cow?'	(A) for Bill's uncle but for Bill it is an instruction in the guise of a question.

Preparation for the next class

On the blackboard the teacher draws
a series of figures which she then covers.

Category and Function

Day 3

Bill brings in the information that was
was asked for in the previous class and
there is a brief discussion and comparison.
The teacher then asks the students to
compare their homework with each other
and to deduce the formula for a
right-angled triangle. She questions:

Q33: 'How did you go about finding   (A)   Recalling, unifying
     that out?'

R17: 'I made it into a rectangle and
     found the two halves were
     the same.'

R18: 'I asked my brother.'

The teacher then gives several right-
angled triangles for them to calculate
area to ensure that everyone under-
stands the principle.

Q34: 'How can we use our knowledge   (B)   Connecting
     of the areas of rectangles and right-
     angled triangles to find the areas
     of the figures on the board?'

She reveals the board:

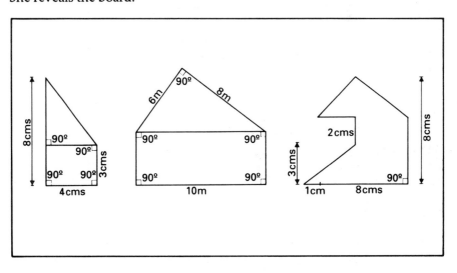

Category and Function

Students work in pairs and check their answers with the teacher. Teacher then says, 'We are now going to work differently. You are a group of settlers who have been granted a large parcel of land. Together you have cleared the land. All of us have worked hard and long.'

(Notice how the teacher 'joins' the class by her use of the words, 'we' and 'us'.)

Q35: 'How could we ensure that the land we have been allotted is divided fairly amongst our seven families?'

(B) and (C) Connecting, critically assessing

She continues:
'In those days they had different scales of measurement from those we use today but, for our purposes, I think it would be more useful to stick with the metric system.'

Q36: 'Would it help if you worked in family groups, or would you rather work individually?'

(A)   Establishing procedure

Students decide to work in family groups and are given maps of the land parcel:

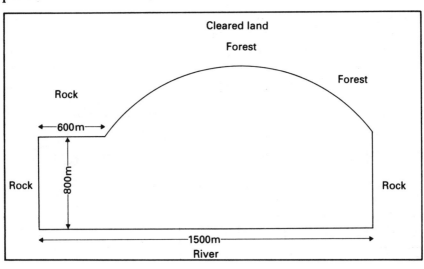

	Category and Function

Q37: 'What is the total cleared area?' (A) Sharing facts
She gets many different answers.
Q38: 'Why do our answers vary?' (B) Interpreting
R19: 'The curves in the map make it
    hard to measure accurately.'
R20: 'Ours is more accurate because we
    made smaller squares so the curve
    is almost a straight line.'

Students eventually agree on a figure
for the total area.
Q39: 'We are seven families. How (B) Connecting
    much land should the families
    receive if there is a fair distribution?'

Students work it out to the nearest
square metre by dividing the total area
by seven.
Q40: 'Now that we know how much
    every family is entitled to, how
    shall we split this land into equal
    parts?' (B) Connecting
R21: 'We could try it and then count
    the squares.'
Q41: 'Do you still want to work in
    families?' (A) Considering ways to
    work

Students agree that this is the most
enjoyable way to work except for one
boy who complains that he is doing
all the work.
Q42: 'I wonder if that same complaint
    would have been made in earlier
    times?' (B) Connecting

The students carry out the task and are
able to find seven approximately equal
lots of land.
    This satisfies the teacher's mathematics'
objectives. However, there is more to
land than square metres and the
teacher's final question is a 'thinker'
question.

	Category and Function
Q43: 'I wonder how the family who drew Lot C will water their cattle?'	(C) Projecting which demands both thought and feeling.

SUMMARY

There is no doubt that in these lessons the teacher's objectives are for her students to learn how to calculate areas and use formulae. There is no doubt, either, that she could have taught all that in one lesson by presenting the formulae and allowing the students to practise them. She would then be able to discover, by testing, how many students had taken in the material, were able to hand it back to her and apply it in different ways. However, it is doubtful whether the majority of students would have the kind of understanding of the principles of the formulae that these students have who, even many years later, remember that particular series of lessons and, what is more, have no difficulty in determining areas! We suggest that this is because, through her questioning, the teacher understood the importance of taking the time to put her students into the material, as well as to bring the material to them.

What ways did the teacher use to bring the material to her students?

- She captured their interest.
- She provided them with tasks that engaged them with the material.
- She varied the pace, making the social health of the class work for her, rather than against her.
- She invited with questions rather than ordering through instructions.
- She gave many opportunities for students to make decisions for the way in which they learned.
- She was honest about what was to be learned.

What ways did the teacher use to put her students into the material?

- She was prepared to take the time for the students to discover for themselves.
- She used a variety of strategies and techniques to create a personal framework for the students.
- Through her teaching, the validity and purpose of the lesson material was proved, not for the students by her, but *by them for themselves*.

- The way in which she structured the questions challenged the students at all levels of competence to think about the material and the situations (or problems) she set up. The questions permitted the students to exercise their feelings as they manipulated the material.

- She offered many opportunities for ownership and for taking control through shared activities and peer teaching.

In summary, here is a teacher who uses the taxonomies as guides for bringing the material to her students; who is prepared to make the time to allow students to find their own relationship with the material; and who enables them to think and feel in many different ways by using all the categories of questions.

You may have noticed that the last question which the teacher asks is defined in the text as a 'thinker' question. Questions themselves can be, and are, defined in many ways. Every definition carries its own 'title' and often there are many different titles given to the same kinds of question. This can be very confusing and so, in the next chapter, we will attempt to pull together the terminology and provide a glossary of questions.

All of these kinds of questions fit into any category of the classification, depending upon what it is you want it to do. If you wanted to deal with procedure (Category A), an example of 'the closed question' (which generally asks for a 'yes' or 'no' answer) might be, 'Now. Free Trade. Are you ready, Lawson?' If you are shaping understanding (Category B), your question might be, 'Can we assume that Free Trade will change our lives?' If you are pressing for reflection (Category C), the question might be, 'Does it matter to you that in the future our vineyards will become theme parks?'

You will note, however, that the last two categories are not very well served by the 'closed' question and that is why knowing the definitions can provide you with a more flexible repertoire of questions.

Chapter 7

A glossary of questions

> Definitions, like questions and metaphors are instruments of thinking. Their authority rests entirely on their usefulness, not their correctness.
>
> (Postman, 1979: 145)

In any reading you have done or in any course you may have taken about teaching, you will probably have been warned against using one kind of question and encouraged to use another kind. People will stress the importance of the 'divergent' question. Professor X will tell (or has told) you never to use the 'covert' question. Doctor Y says that 'covert' questions are the key to discovery learning and everyone agrees that the key to effective questioning is the use of the 'key' question!

Many questions have different names for the same or similar functions (the 'heuristic', the 'creative' and the 'freeing', for example) and some names are umbrellas – the 'open' question covers such questions as the 'reflective', the 'divergent', the 'hypothetical' – and so on. You may know different names for the questions we will describe because you have read different books and been taught by different teachers. There is a staggering breadth of terminology and we have selected some fifty terms for definition. The order is designed to maintain your interest and not to suggest an hierarchical approach.

Higher-order questions are those which ask for analysis, synthesis or evaluation, the last three categories of 'Bloom's taxonomy' which define these as demanding more complex and thus 'higher' levels of thinking. For example:

Analysis:
'Why is it so important for different cultural groups in our society to maintain their cultural heritage?'
Synthesis:
'For the end-of-the-year concert, what theme could we look at that would best express the wide variety of cultures in our school?'
Evaluation:
'What significance has the government's decision to opt for the concept of the "cultural mosaic" over the "melting pot" for today's society?'

Lower-order questions are those which ask for knowledge, comprehension and application, the first three categories of 'Bloom's taxonomy', which defines these as demanding less complex and thus 'lower' levels of thinking. For example:

Knowledge:
'How many different cultural groups are represented in our classroom?'
Comprehension:
'What do we mean by the cultural mosaic?'
Application:
'What other examples of cultural policy promote social "ghettoization"?'

The closed question is
(a) one which asks for the short, right answer:
   'What was the political system in Germany in 1933–45?', or
(b) one which may be answered by 'yes' or 'no' and can be recognized by
   the use of the interrogative structure of verb/noun, for example: 'is it?',
   'have you?', 'will you?', 'shall we?':
      'Have you done your homework?'

For anything further to happen another question has to be posed. The closed question is very useful for testing recall, focusing attention, obtaining information and for moving on quickly when you wish to avoid discussion. It is often a way of helping reluctant students into talk because it does not ask them to put anything of themselves into the answer.

The open question is one which suggests that the teacher does not have one particular answer in mind but is inviting students to consider and advance many possibilities. This kind of question is 'open' to many answers:
   'What kinds of things can the government do for the homeless?'

The overt and *the covert question* are those which are designed to elicit feeling responses.

The overt question is direct and can sometimes be seen as threatening; it generally produces a short answer:
   'How are you feeling?'
   'Were you afraid?'
   'Would you like to . . .?'
   'Why didn't you do your homework?'

The covert question is indirect and invites elaboration; it often masquerades as a statement:
   'What is in your mind?'
   'What are your concerns?'
   'How might one describe that experience?'
   'It must be difficult to hold a job and keep up with your school work?'

The polar question is one which asks the question to which the answer must either be 'yes' or 'no'; 'true' or 'false'. It is used extensively in

questionnaires which are hoping to 'polarize' or unify opinion and there is no chance for 'maybe', 'sometimes' or 'it depends':
    'Is butter bad for you?'

The branching question is one which gives students a choice between alternatives:
    'Shall we do this . . . or that . . .?'
    'Will it be either . . . or . . .?'
    'Shall we get help or try it on our own?'

The confrontation question or *the 'tough' question* is one which attempts to eliminate inconsistency and challenges the validity of what has been said or done. Graves (1983) suggests that such a question causes in the student 'a temporary loss of control' because it challenges the validity of what he has been engaged upon or the logic of what he has been saying (or writing); which is not to say that you should not challenge a student's thinking when the need for clarification arises:
    'A few minutes ago you said that the Native people of northern Quebec should have sole rights over their territories and now you say that Quebec Hydro should be allowed to build dams there. How do you explain this contradiction?'

The key question or *the critical question* is one which opens up the issue:
    'I don't suppose it matters, does it, if mentally handicapped students don't learn anything in the integrated classroom, provided they have the social experience?'

The deductive and *the inductive question* We have talked to a lot of intelligent people about the difference between these two kinds of questions with the following results:
    If the question is *deductive,* the statement in the question has to be accepted and the answerers' job is to prove it:
        'Cinderella is a classic fairy tale. What are the characteristics of a fairy tale?'

    If the question is *inductive,* the answerer will have to look at a series of instances and encompass them in an answer:
        'What are the characteristics of a classic fairy tale?'

We often teach through the deductive process without realizing its implications. How many adults think of Hamlet only as a man who couldn't make up his mind? Deductive reasoning can be limiting because all you will be looking for in Shakespeare's text is where it supports or refutes that opinion; the chances are that you will overlook the other aspects of Hamlet's character which might cause you to think very differently about him. On the other hand, by asking, 'What kind of man was Hamlet?' the student can bring his experiences and his feelings, as well as his knowledge of the text, into his answer. More difficult to mark, of course!

To clarify: *the deductive question* is one which confines the area of inquiry. It is, as Weingartner (1977: 12–14) points out, reductive, convergent and closes down. *The inductive question* is one which widens the process of inquiry. It is expansive, divergent and opens up. If, as Hunkins (1974: 9) says, 'inductive and deductive thinking are complementary parts of a continuous cognitive process', then it becomes important to know which you are using and why you are using it.

Questions which require a written reply tend to be deductive rather than inductive because the answers are easier to mark. The questions confine the area. They must be carefully planned because you won't be there to rephrase if they are ambiguous. Written questions usually follow the statement/question format:
'Caesar was said to be ambitious. What evidence in Shakespeare's Julius Caesar do you have to support or refute this statement?'

The heuristic question or *the creative question* is one which guides the student into discovering the answer for himself through all his resources (knowledge, experience, imagination and feelings):
'Now we know all the facts about our situation, what are the implications for each one of you?'

The educative or *productive question* is one which is designed to help students learn, leading them to new facts, new perspectives and new ideas:
'If we were to be part of an expedition to a new planet, what kind of people would we need to be?'

The freeing question is one where the teacher clearly 'signals' there is no one right answer; the student is free to wonder:
'I wonder what happened to unicorns?'
(Our favourite answer is, 'Only one got into the Ark'.)

The hypothetical question is one which frees the responder to 'let his imagination run wild'; for example, this favourite essay topic for 10–14 year olds:
'What would you do with a million dollars?'
There is sometimes a problem with this kind of question in that it demands a creative response, but because the question lacks a focus, it can produce unstructured and unfocused answers. Try:
'How would you spend a bequest of a million dollars for the benefit of the community?'

The divergent question is one which invites many different responses from a large number of students and encourages both concrete and abstract thinking:
'What might happen in a hospital if the water system became contaminated?'

The factual question is one which requires students to give information:
'How is oxygen absorbed by the blood?'

The recall question asks a student to draw from his knowledge or experience. This is the most popular/infamous and/or ubiquitous question in the teaching lexicon:
'What did Margaret just say, Duncan?'
'What is a right-angled triangle?'

The research question is one which not only invites the students into research but also invites them to assume responsibility for designing the procedure for the research:
'How could we find out how to measure the weight of the earth?'

The enactive question is one which drives the responder into further thought and/or direct action:
'What are we going to do about it?'

The social question is so-called because it is used as part of classroom management and as a means of pulling the group together:
'Aren't we straying beyond the point?'

The rhetorical question is one which is designed to affect the emotions and does not expect an answer:
'Who amongst you has not sinned?' (Guilt)
'Who cares?' (Deflation)

The 'thinker' question is one which, like the rhetorical, evokes emotion and does not require an answer. It should also generate thought. It is generally asked at the end of the lesson in the hope that students will think about it before the next lesson. It is often prefaced with 'I wonder . . .?', 'Do you suppose that . . .?':
'I wonder how the family who drew Lot C will water their cattle?'

The reflective question is one which clearly signals that an immediate answer is not required; that the teacher is prepared to wait; that it is acceptable to think aloud and there need be no resolution nor consensus:
'Can you remember a time when your future depended upon someone you didn't trust?'

The opening question (Graves, 1983) is not to be confused with the 'open' question. It is designed to open up dialogue between teacher and student(s). It has to do with the teacher's ability to recognize the student's mood in order to help him move into the work:
'How is it going, Ted?'
'What are all of you intending to do now?'

The following question (Graves, 1983) is one which reflects what has just been said by the student in order to help him to hear what he has just said:

Student: 'We should stop letting foreigners into our country.'

Teacher: 'You think that we should keep all foreigners out?'

The intention here is the implied question, 'Are you saying . . .?' You must avoid correcting, changing the language or infusing your own biases by your tone of voice. This is a 'mirroring' technique, as Graves points out, and is used extensively in counselling.

The synopsis question is one which is designed to help students to crystalize their thinking 'up to this point':

'Where did we get to yesterday?'

'What are the important points to come out of this discussion?'

The clarifying question invites the student to elaborate a somewhat bald statement; to refine a rather 'woolly' comment:

'Can you be more specific?'

'Am I right in thinking . . .?'

The process question or *the development question* is that question which asks the student to look at the steps from the beginning of the task to arrive where he is presently, in order to help him discover for himself where he should go next or for him to see how a particular activity has helped him to move forward:

'What have you been doing up 'til now?'

'Why don't you look at how you got this far?'

The evaluating question invites students to look at their work in a critical fashion:

'What did you learn from this?'

'What new skills have you acquired?'

'How does this compare with your work last term?'

'How valid are our conclusions?'

The silly question is that question which is not asked because the person who would like to ask it thinks it would make him 'look silly'. If you need to know something, then you are silly not to ask the question which will help you to find out!

The 'stupid' question is that question which someone has the courage but not the confidence to ask. It is generally prefaced with:

'I know I sound stupid but . . . '.

The leading question is one in which the question tells, strongly implies or prompts the answer that is being sought:

'Would you not say that the fog made it difficult for an accurate identification of the alleged assailant?'

The serialized or 'machine gun' question is one which gives the student no opportunity to think for himself before alternatives are thrust at him:
    'If you were going to university, would you enrol at Queen's? How about York? Or Western? Or Simon Fraser?'

The marathon question is one which is long and involved and students often lose the thread:
    'What do you think we should do about Free Trade with the USA – keep out competition from other countries by raising tariffs on their produce, even if this means we don't have as much foreign trade or try to increase our trade with other countries by agreeing with them to lower our tariffs if they lower theirs?'

The ambiguous question is one which leaves the student unsure of what to reply to or how his answer, if he has one, will be interpreted. It is often followed by 'or not':
    'Do you think Canada should supply arms to Third World countries or not?'
    If the student says 'yes', does he mean 'Yes, I think we should' or 'Yes, I think we shouldn't'? This question is 'closed' and an intuitive realization of this leads to the 'or not' being tagged on. This, however, does not make the question 'open' but merely impossible to answer (which will not prevent students from trying).

The double-barrelled question is one where a bias (generally subconscious) intrudes on the question:
    'Do you prefer a story that is short and well-written or one which is long and frivolous?'
    They may prefer something short and frivolous!

The prompt or elicitation question is accompanied by 'heavy' clues which are to be found in the wording of the question, the intonation or the pauses to be filled in by students:
    'This is a. . .?'
    'The knife is. . .(sharp, indrawn breath). . .?'
    'We should remember to be. . .? . . .when we are using knives.'
    Edwards and Mercer (1987: 105) warn us that the problem with questions like this is 'that they can give a false impression of the extent to which the students understand what they are saying and doing'.

The contrapuntal question
    'James – you remember that experiment, the one I was referring to, not the one in January – that was a mistake on my part – the one in February, the experiment which is referred to in your text? You know the one I'm talking about, there's no mistake about it, is there? Now, during that experiment there were three of you present. You, Pam, Ricky and Leslie

– no that makes four, I'm sorry. There were four people present and what I want to ask you, James, is did any of you during that experiment – any one or more of you, I mean you or Pam or Rick or Leslie – I think there was no one else present. Now, James, this is very important, I shall make a note of your answer – did you, or Pam or Rick or Leslie – any one of you, I mean – write anything like this – I don't mean the actual words – no one expects you to remember the exact words all that time ago, but anything of the kind, I mean? I'm waiting for your answer, James.'

Need we say anything more?

The why question There is some controversy about the value of 'why' questions. Many educators and most psychologists suggest that 'why' questions should be avoided 'like the plague'. In part, we agree when these can be perceived as a tool to destroy confidence or to suggest disapproval, objections or criticism:
   'Why would you say that?' (prying into personal life)
   'Why did you do that?' (criticizing personal choice)
   'Why do you always wear that colour?' (attacking the way one presents oneself)
   Dillon (1983: 30–1) suggests 'from long experience, children have learned that there is, in fact, no meaningful answer to a "why" question', for example:
   'Why haven't you done your homework?'
   The student knows that the questioner is not interested in the answer but is using the question as a means to inform the student of her displeasure and/or frustration.
   On the other hand, 'why' is the great educational question. It is the way in which we learn; it drives us to discover our world. We all ask 'why' questions but it is *the way* in which a 'why' question is asked that changes it from a perceived personal interrogation of the respondent to being seen as a genuine need to know on the part of the questioner.

The everyday question is one which comes readily to mind and often springs thoughtlessly from the lips as part of a kind of ritual dialogue which serves a social function and often does not expect or get an answer (or at any rate a detailed answer!):
   'How are you?'
   'What have you been doing?'
   'What have I done with my glasses?'

And then there are:

The unanswerable questions The 'unanswerable' questions are those which are the eternal questions of existence:
   'Who am I? Why am I here? What is truth?' These are the questions of

the very young child but they are also questions of tremendous interest to adolescents and are usually initiated by them when the context is right. It is a signal to those questioned of an ability and a need to reason in abstractions.

Northrop Frye (1988: 192) writes that 'Heidigger says the first question of philosophy, and the hardest to answer because it's also the simplest, is: Why is there something rather than nothing?'

Before we leave these definitions of question terminology, there is one other term with which you should be familiar.

Recitation   This has nothing to do with reciting *La Belle Dame Sans Merci*. It is a classroom procedure in which 'the teacher asks a question, the student gives an answer, the teacher evaluates the answer, and in the same breath, asks another question' (Dillon, 1988b: 85). In this procedure the teacher controls the discourse; there is little time for considering the answers (your own and others) and the constant evaluation of answers is extremely inhibiting. We most strongly urge you to avoid this procedure.

There is one more thing: there are certain teacher questions which would be dangerous for the student to answer! For example: *'How many times have I told you that?'*

ALTERNATIVES TO QUESTIONS

Statements which are really questions   You will have noticed that some of the sample questions we have used in earlier chapters look more like statements than they do questions. Statements often take the place of questions and are valuable additions to a questioning repertoire. They work extremely well, providing that students understand that a statement is offered as an invitation for discussion and not as something which cannot be disputed.

A *declarative statement*   is used to express a thought and to generate an exploration of that thought. It conveys information and it does not prescribe what kind and how much response is expected:
   'I see no reason why 15-year-old children can't be recruited to fight for their country.'
   Four studies between 1972 and 1983 suggest that responses to teacher statements may be 'both longer and more complex than responses to questions' (Dillon, 1988b: 137).

A *reflective restatement*   is used to summarize and synthesize what a speaker has just said. It can be used to encourage a student to elaborate upon his original contribution, and as a way of suggesting that, if there is a misunderstanding, it is on the part of the listener rather than inadequacy or confusion on the part of the speaker.

A reflective restatement often begins with phrases such as:
'I understand you to say that . . . '
'You mean that . . . '
'What you are saying is . . . '
For example:
Student: 'Well, like it seems to me that . . . I mean there are some things that people shouldn't be allowed to pass on – like this friend of mine who got a kind of blood poisoning in hospital, you know . . .?'
Teacher: 'You are saying that we need more efficient ways of analysing blood.'
Student: 'Well, maybe. But what I was really meaning was that people with these kinds of diseases should be put away.'
This teacher's reflective restatement enabled the student to clarify for himself and for the teacher and the class what it was he really meant, which led to a very lively discussion indeed!

A 'state of mind' statement is used to express a state of mind or feeling. It often begins with phrases such as:
'I'm not sure I am coping with . . . '
'I don't feel comfortable with . . . '
'I'm not sure I know enough about . . . '
It allows students to see that the teacher is human and suffers from the same confusions and difficulties as they do. Most importantly, it removes the teacher from being 'the one who always *can* to being the one who sometimes *can't*'. It invites students to elaborate, to help and sometimes to direct.

An invitational statement is used to invite a student to elaborate. It is often prefaced with such phrases as:
'I'd like to hear more about . . . ' rather than 'What else . . .?', or
'I'd be interested in knowing . . . ' instead of 'Who knows . . .?'.
An invitational statement demonstrates the teacher's personal interest in a student's contribution and is most effective on a one-to-one basis because it gives value to what was said and the experience that prompted it.

And then there is always 'the other way around'
The question which should be a statement
'Don't you think it would be helpful if you studied more?' which is really the statement,
'You'd get higher marks if you studied more.'

The instruction which masquerades as a question
'Shall we get into groups of four?'
'Groups of four, please' is faster, cleaner and more to the point!
These kinds of question–statements and question–instructions are often used when a teacher wants to appear democratic instead of authoritative.

They are widely used by student teachers who are anxious for student approval of their instructions. Have they ever thought of the consequences if the students said, 'No!' out loud?

Perhaps, at this point, you are thinking of giving up asking questions entirely and have decided to join a telephone answering service. Don't hand in your resignation yet.

In Chapter 5 we presented a classification of questions made up of three categories. Each category had a function – *pulling out* (Category A), *filling in* (Category B) and *extending* (Category C) – and each general function had a number of particular functions.

A function can be performed by many tools. So, too, there are many kinds of questions for every category. It is not necessary for you, every time you plan or ask a question, to identify that question by name, but knowing the names of questions and what they do does make it easier to analyse your questions and those of others and to help your students understand and use them. Whatever the question you ask, whatever its kind and function, the first guide in asking questions is think about *how the question will help students engage in (feeling) and with (thought) the material.*

Questions do not operate in a vacuum. You and your students need to work with an 'open' agenda where they see their relationship with you as collaborative and teaching not as a didactic transmission of pre-formulated knowledge but as an attempt to negotiate shared meanings and understandings (Edwards and Westgate, 1987: 174–5). It is often a long process to arrive at the point where students are ready to accept that without their contributions the work cannot proceed; that the teacher is prepared to wait for answers because she recognizes that questions need to be considered and that thoughtful answers need time for formulation.

In the next chapter we set that context by looking at the characteristics of effective classroom interaction: the nature of classroom discourse; the characteristics of effective classroom discourse and the power of 'active' silence.

Part III

How do we question?

Chapter 8

Fewer questions, better questions and time to think

> To conceive an educative question requires thought;
> To formulate it requires labour;
> To pose it, tact.
> None of this is mysterious
> And all of it is within our reach.
>
> (Dillon, 1983: 8)

The classic concept of learning is that it occurs when the teacher asks the questions and the students can answer them, but the reality is that learning does not occur until the learner needs to know and can formulate the question for himself.

We must recognize that however indispensable as teachers we consider ourselves, children have been learning by themselves and asking questions since they were born. 'We are by nature question-asking, answer-making, problem-solving animals and we are extremely good at it, above all when we are little', says John Holt (1982: 189). We must not allow our students to lose this natural ability by ignoring it. Classroom interaction is the activity which sets students into the process of inquiry (thinking, feeling, discussing, arguing, philosophizing, etc.) and the teacher is, most often, the initiator of the action.

The place of the teacher, Vygotsky and Bruner suggest, is central as a guide to effective learning (Bruner, 1986). The job of the teacher is to open doors; to let students know that doors exist, that there are many of them, that they are meant to be opened (some easily, some with difficulty) and that there is something beyond every door that is worthwhile knowing about. The key to the door, to carry the analogy further is, most often, the 'good' question.

When something is put into words it promotes control of the knowledge that is expressed and, suggests Woods (1987), speaking those words can be the 'essential moment of appropriation and re-interpretation which helps establish ownership'. Questioning generates the kind of talk and communication which can lead to learning; questioning reveals to the teacher the readiness of students to take control; and questioning (by both students and teacher) establishes the cultural nature of the classroom. And it is the nature of the discourse which dictates the quality of the learning.

CLASSROOM DISCOURSE

The basic difference between a large number of people engaged in social conversation and students engaged in traditional educational discourse is one of organization. When we engage in free-flowing conversation in a social situation, we talk in pairs or in small groups and these groupings dissolve and reform as the topics of conversation develop or change. It is our interest, as individuals, in the content which controls the organization.

In the classroom our 'conversations' embrace everyone in the class at the same time. In order to maintain a focus, to assure that everyone has a chance to contribute (the silent to be jogged into speech, the verbose to be eased into silence), we need someone to take control: that 'someone' is, 99 per cent of the time, the teacher. The effect is to put the teacher at the centre of the 'conversation', through whom everything passes and by whom students expect everything to be mediated. There is nothing wrong with this when it is important for everyone to share a common basis of information or when the teacher wants to assess how much the students know, but it is not the kind of classroom discourse we are talking about here.

What students contribute and the way in which the talk is advanced is drawn directly from their background, experience and prior knowledge – their 'personal luggage'. It is these frames of reference against which the new information is assessed ('what's that got to do with me?') and measured ('how important is that to me?') and through which new information and experience can be absorbed, internalized and owned. As early as 1958, research was demonstrating that a knowledge of students' backgrounds made a 'significant difference in a teacher's effectiveness as measured by students' learning' (McKeachie, 1978: 38). Productive classroom discourse gives students opportunities to make connections with their own lives; to be responsible for the organization of that discourse (who speaks and when, who asks questions and so on) and it allows them to participate in controlling the process (what ideas are introduced and developed). To Britton (1970: 239–40) this is 'an important mode of learning'; 'Participants profit from their own talking . . . from what others contribute and, above all, from the interaction – that is to say, from the enabling effect of each upon the others.' (For an analysis of talk, discourse and discussion, see Appendix 1.)

CHARACTERISTICS OF EFFECTIVE CLASSROOM DISCOURSE

It takes time to promote effective classroom discourse and you should be aware that:

1 Discourse depends for its intelligibility upon the gradual accumulation of shared contexts of talk and experience which build 'joint frames of reference' (Edwards and Mercer, 1987: 65). Talk is a way of sorting out

ideas. Thought shapes language and language shapes thought and both are necessary in the cognitive, social and emotional development of students.

2   Discourse can give students practice in making questions and assessing their 'impact' and should be an opportunity for them to control and direct the exchange of ideas. Within the larger discourse small conversations will occur; these are natural and an important means of 'scaffolding'[1].

3   In this kind of discourse the rhythm of the dialogue is similar to the rhythm of the students' own peer talk which, Britton (1970: 243) suggests, 'rests upon a general consensus of opinion and attitude, yet individual differences are expressed. It is exploratory ... it penetrates deeper ... than a more structured, more objective analysis could have taken them.' When thought and feeling are focused and given expression, they cannot always be stopped by the ringing of a bell or a change of environment. Productive discourse can have a 'spill-over' effect which often involves the participants continuing the 'conversation' outside the classroom, with you, other teachers and parents and friends.

In enabling discourse, you should consider that:

1   The arrangement of the classroom plays a significant part in the success of the discourse by enabling everyone to be in a position to 'read' the non-verbal signals in conjunction with what is being said.

2   Your own personal luggage (which includes your biases, attitudes and values) can be used constructively and openly as part of the development of the discourse, rather than as censor, control and directive.

3   Your role will change from the position of the holder of knowledge and only controller of its revelations to that of a facilitator of learning – one who has a place, but not a central place, in the dialogue.

4   Finally, you must recognize that, because students have permission to talk, there will be ideas and attitudes expressed which will conflict with and trespass on others' concepts and feelings (and, sometimes or often, upon your own). Northrop Frye (1988: 184) warns that 'as long as we have the words to formulate ideas with, those ideas will still be potential, and potentially dangerous.' But effective discourse has its own built-in discipline which comes from a sense of responsibility of the individual to the group and of the group to the individual and from a common commitment to the task.

Just as we have looked at the characteristics of effective classroom discourse in order to establish a climate in which discourse can flourish, let us now examine the characteristics of effective questioning. To illustrate this, both in this chapter and later on, we will take a source that was used with general students, aged 16/17. The teacher's focus: *To strive against great odds and not win the prize*, was chosen because it matched the students' experience. Sometimes it is more effective to illustrate a point with a negative example and we let you know when we are doing so, although by this time we are pretty sure you will be able to decide that for yourself.

Source:

> Captain Robert Scott and his party of five left base camp in Antarctica in October, 1911, with motor sledges, ponies and dogs, in their bid to be the first at the South Pole. The motors soon broke down, the ponies, unable to cope with the extreme cold, were shot and the dogs sent back to base because Scott was not prepared to sacrifice them. The polar party, themselves pulling the sleds, arrived at the Pole in January, 1912, to find that they had been forestalled by the Norwegian explorer, Amundsen. The weather on the return journey was exceptionally bad. Evans, the group doctor, died and Captain Oates sacrificed himself by walking out into a blizzard while his companions slept. The three survivors struggled on but were confined at their next camp for nine days by the blizzard and all perished. Their frozen bodies were found by search parties in November, 1912.

CHARACTERISTICS OF A GOOD QUESTION

A good question is an expressive demonstration of a genuine curiosity; behind every question there must be the intention to know:
  'I wonder what drives men to risk their lives in pointless adventure?'

A good question has an inner logic related in some way to the teacher's focus and the students' experiences; a negative example might be:
  'When Scott saw the Norwegian flag at the South Pole, what did he say to his men?'
What would your answer be? Would it be printable?

In a good question the words are ordered in such a way that the thinking is clarified both for the students and the teacher; again an 'ambiguous' example:
  'Are you in favour of his not going at all, or his not taking dogs to the Pole?
What is the question here? Is it,
  'What would their chances have been had they kept the dogs instead of pulling the sleds themselves?' Or is the teacher asking,
'Should someone who leads a perilous expedition allow his personal biases to endanger the lives of others?'

In a good question the intent must be supported by intonation and non-verbal signals. The pace of the question should match the intent:

Teacher *(bright and sparkling, speaking quickly)*: 'I wonder why Captain Oates would do a thing like that?'

or

Teacher *(speaking slowly and almost to herself)*: 'I wonder . . . why Captain Oates . . . would do a thing like that?'

Can you hear the difference?

A good question can provide surprise. Students will sometimes respond to a good question by talking about things that neither they nor the teacher were aware that they knew:

'Have you ever, at any time, risked someone else's life?'

Students were amazed to discover how often they had, unwittingly, done just this. Although it did not directly 'fit' the teacher's focus, an important discussion developed on the morality of responsibility and the fear of being thought a coward.

A good question challenges existing thinking and encourages reflection:

'What makes a hero?'

Students began defining a hero by referring to film actors. A stimulating conversation followed about whether someone who creates the *illusion* of heroism can be called a hero.

A good question is seen as part of an on-going dialogue which involves relationships between speakers. A negative example:

'John's ideas are somewhat anachronistic. Who can put him right?'

Who would dare to keep this dialogue going?

A good question has reason, focus, clarity and appropriate intonation. It can challenge and surprise but should not be seen as a weapon by which to diminish others. A good question maintains student engagement, stimulates thought and evokes feelings.

WHAT IS IT THAT PROMOTES DEEPER THINKING AND ANSWERS OF SUBSTANCE?

The three interdependent components of the responding process are: listening, thinking and hearing one's own answer.

Characteristics of active listening

● Active listeners are genuinely interested in the reply and willing to let it change them in some way (Laidlaw, 1989).

- Active listeners are prepared to wait for answers.
- Active listeners are as interested in the responses of others as they are in their own.
- Active listeners are in tune with the social context of the classroom as well as the subject content.

Characteristics of quality thinking time

- Quality thinking time depends upon everyone being comfortable with silence.
- Quality thinking time depends upon everyone being *seen* to be comfortable with silence.
- Quality thinking time is filled with the energy of curiosity which will be balanced by the energy of thinking and feeling. Active silence speaks as loudly as words. An interrupted silence is equal to interrupting a speaker; thought is part of verbal expression and exchange.

Characteristics of thoughtful answers

- A thoughtful answer can move the exploration on to a new stage.
- A thoughtful answer can raise the exploration to a higher intellectual and emotional level.
- A thoughtful answer shows respect for the question.
- A thoughtful answer may not come easily; it may be marked with hesitancy and rephrasing (Barnes, 1976).
- A thoughtful answer reveals the level of thought and feeling in the responder.
- A thoughtful answer often appears in the form of a question.
- A thoughtful answer depends upon the care with which the question is put.

The art of questioning involves not only the ability to make and deliver good questions, it also involves active listening, thoughtful answers and, of equal importance, time to think. The key to good questioning is *quality* not quantity.

WHY DO TEACHERS ASK SO MANY QUESTIONS?

If statistics are to be believed (and we can see no reason for not believing them as they confirm our own experience!), teachers do ask far too many questions. Some ask between 300 and 400 questions on an average day. When you eliminate the times when students are busy at other things, for example, desk work, reading, recess, PE, eating and so on, this means teachers are asking a question every 5.6 to 11.0 seconds (Primary English Notes, n.d.).

Why?

- Is it because we believe that the more questions we ask, the more possibilities there are for learning?
- Is it because our view of ourselves as professionals endows us with the right and responsibility to ask questions and our view of students grants them the right and responsibility to give answers?
- Is it because we like talking more than listening?
- Is it because we have read that a good teacher asks questions, so we assume that by asking a lot of questions we will be better than just 'good'?
- Is it because, as Benjamen (1981: 71) suggests, '[our] questions seem to keep [us] afloat; take them away and [we] would sink'?
- Is it because we use our questions to ensure that students understand that 'we are the authority, the expert and that only *we* know what is important and relevant for them'? (Benjamen, 1981: 72).
- Is it because we use our questions to check attention, assess rote learning, test knowledge, control topics of discussion and direct students' thought and action (Edwards and Mercer, 1987)?
- Is it because the more questions we ask, the more hope we think we have for 'coming up with a good one'?

There is a lot of truth in these question-answers: learning, as we have said, does occur as the result of questions; questions do serve to focus the objectives of the curriculum; a good teacher *is* a good questioner and statistics suggest that, for many teachers, questioning is indeed the central technique. But a teacher is not a vacuum cleaner salesman who is told that the more calls he makes the more likely he is to make a sale. Although we might make an argument for the question as a 'house call on the mind', the analogy must stop there! Questioning is far too important for you to rely on the 'scatter-gun' approach and far too valuable a technique for you not to know what you are about when you are using it. The art of questioning involves not only the ability to make and deliver good questions, it also involves answering. Where in this fusillade of questions is there room for the answer? Where is the time for students to think about answers, to choose the words to frame the answers and to speak the answers or to frame and articulate their questions? Where is the time for the teacher to consider the answers and to formulate her response to those answers?

THINKING TIME

'What is truth?' said jesting Pilate and would not stay for an answer.'
(Sir Francis Bacon; quoted in Cambridge, 1949: 1)

Silence is a deliberate act by the teacher that encourages thought and response.
(Dillon, 1983: 38)

'Wait time' is a term which is used to refer to what the teacher is doing after she has asked a question. But, in a classroom which is built upon the principles of active participation, we believe that 'thinking time' more properly describes what is happening.

In the theatre, there are many words to indicate what is happening to the actor when the action is stilled: 'pause', 'silence', 'waits', 'listens', 'thinks', 'holds', 'looks', 'stops'. These words do not mean that the internal (or dramatic) action has stopped but rather that the expressive activity stops in order for the audience to become more aware of what is going on in the minds and hearts of the characters. These silences are filled with the actions of thoughts and feelings. So, too, the classroom when silence occurs. Thinking and feeling are internal activities which take energy and need time.

The teacher's ability to wait calmly while students consider the question and formulate the answer:

- builds trust in the relationship between teacher and students;
- gives time for students to look at the question from many angles;
- frees them to provide answers of substance;
- presses them to respond by speaking what is on and in their minds;
- suggests that they share the responsibility for their learning; and
- increases student-to-student interaction and student-to-teacher responses.

How long should you wait?

A Faculty of Education student handout states that you should 'allow a pause time after you ask a question (3 seconds at least)'. How long is three seconds? Not long, is it? Would you be surprised to learn that it is *two seconds longer* than most teachers wait for a response to their questions?

There are many statistics on the timing of what is called 'question recitation'. Even taking a generous view of these statistics, we find that if one question is asked every 10 seconds (six questions per minute) it is expected that: the teacher asks the question; the students think, formulate and one student speaks the answer; and the teacher absorbs, considers and weaves the answer back into the lesson context and focus – all in the time frame of ten seconds. This means that the question will have to be short, direct and lower-order, requiring an answer which is also short, direct and uncomplicated by complex thought or feeling, resulting in a communication which is immediately applicable to the teacher's lesson plan. However many questions are asked per minute, the 'thinking time' given by teachers has almost always been recorded as not more than one second. If an answer is 'not forthcoming within that second, teachers [tend] to repeat or rephrase the question, ask a different question or call on another student'. Furthermore, Purkey goes on, 'when a student make[s] an initial response, teachers [tend] to react within one second with praise, an additional question or some other interjection (Purkey, 1978: 73).

Why is it so hard to wait?

The nature of social discourse lacks silence and in any conversational 'lull' we remember the old social dictum, 'Keep the conversational ball rolling!'. We are not used to productive and constructive silence within everyday talk, 'dead air' on the radio makes us anxious and there is never 'nothing going on' on TV unless the set breaks down. Our natural reaction in the classroom when a silence falls is discomfort and, sometimes, fear – fear that we have asked a poor question, that the students don't know the answer or that the silence will act as an invitation for the students to fill it with something irrelevant (a fart, a smart-aleck remark and so on).

When we do have the courage to increase 'thinking time', research demonstrates that significant changes occur:

- students give longer answers,
- more students volunteer answers,
- more questions are asked by students,
- student responses are more analytical, creative and evaluative, and students report that, 'Class is more interesting' (Ferrara, 1981).

Isn't all this worth 'waiting' for?

You may wonder if there is anything more to say about asking questions? We think it might be helpful to suggest some techniques from which you can draw those which will best serve your own particular classroom style. Because we are hoping to address a broad range of styles, this chapter looks, perhaps, more formidable than it really is!

Chapter 9

Putting the question, handling the answer

In the previous chapter we talked about creating a psychological atmosphere for promoting effective questioning. We will begin here by looking at the general teaching requirements and techniques by which a teacher can help to establish an environment in which questions and answers become partners in a process of inquiry.

GENERAL TEACHING REQUIREMENTS

1. Classroom arrangement

You need to be aware of the arrangement of the classroom and your place in it. Staying at your desk with students arranged in rows facing you, is not always appropriate for generating different kinds of discourse.

All students should be in a position where they can see and hear and make eye contact with one another, so that participation is both encouraged and made easier.

You should be in a position to 'catch' students' eyes because it is a way to invite response non-verbally. At the same time, you don't want to be 'locked in'. You need to be able to move around the classroom in order to step aside from a controlling position or to provide support by standing by a speaker.

2. Classroom conduct

You need to establish the rituals for 'permission to speak'. In some circumstances you will need a raised hand; in others, particularly in free-flowing classroom discourse, it is important to establish and reinforce the organic discipline of the talk which should not require formal 'permission to speak'.

You need to establish an atmosphere of general respect for the ideas and opinions of others which will, of course, be modelled by your attention and interest in your students' contributions.

3. Lesson focus/objectives

You need to be able to recognize that the questions you have prepared may not be appropriate to the direction in which the discourse is moving; you must be able to restructure them in terms of the on-going talk or else put them aside in order to pose questions which are more relevant.

4. Observation

You need to ensure that in any dialogue (either between you and a student or between students) you find opportunities to throw the subject open to the whole group.

You need to be observant in order to pose questions that otherwise might not be considered; to pick up the *sotto voce* answer; to pick up the mood of the group; to be alert to 'un-voiced answers' and to be able to distinquish the 'smart-aleck' answer from the answer based on a genuine misunderstanding.

5. Voice and intonation

You must be aware of the need for variety in the pattern of the discourse. There is a tendency in all people to 'pick up on' the speech patterns of the previous speaker and it is your responsibility to be conscious of this and to ensure that the vitality of the internal understanding is encouraged and student engagement is maintained.

You must be aware of how your intonations can change the meaning of what you are saying. It is not *what* words you say but *how* you say them which has the most significant personal impact. For example:
'That is all the information you have found?'
could mean, depending on your intonation:

(a) 'There isn't any more?'
(b) 'The resource centre is even more inadequate than I thought!'
(c) 'There is more and you've been too lazy to find it!'
(d) 'Other people have been able to find more.'
(e) 'Perhaps I gave you insufficient directions.'

Try asking the example question aloud, using the intentions (a) through (e) and hear the differences.

GENERAL TEACHING TECHNIQUES

1. Language

You should recognize that, in asking a question, you need to use simple, clear direct language which allows students to connect with the thinking and the feeling behind the words. A question cloaked in complicated grammatical structure and 'high-sounding' language rarely produces high-level, well-expressed thinking.

The words you use and the way in which you use them in your questions will put the student inside the language of the material and of the subject so that the language he uses in response will be appropriate to the content. When a student joins you by answering, he is joining in the process of the inquiry with you and he wants to discover how to manipulate the language of the subject. As Postman (1979: 149) says, 'knowledge of the language of [a] subject ... includes not only what its words mean but, far more important, *how* its words mean. As one learns the language of a subject, one is also learning what the subject is.'

2. Elevating language

Students can think in complexities but they often use language poorly because:

(a) they are simply careless, or the teacher has been careless in the ways she uses language;

(b) they do not have the grammatical skills and/or the vocabulary;

(c) they do not possess the vocabulary of the subject discipline;

(d) they have experienced using language informationally, but lack experience in using language interactively and expressively (Little, 1983).

Teachers, when engaged in discourse have many opportunities to model a variety of language uses without being seen to be critical and correcting. For example (we are using the 'Scott' source from Chapter 8):

'In Norwegian history of Antarctic exploration, what reference might there be to Scott's expedition?'
Student: 'That he messed up!'
Teacher: 'Yes, it could be considered a failure by them.'

Function: To accept the idea and upgrade the language in a way which students can accept without taking offence. We should warn you that upgrading and rephrasing every student's response is as misdirected as constantly repeating their answers!

3. Giving an answer weight

Often in discourse a student will respond in a non-public way, as an 'aside', or he will respond unthinkingly. These remarks are sometimes very valuable and a listening teacher can pick them up and give them weight. For example:

Student (*to another student 'sotto voce'*): 'We certainly wasted a lot of time on a failure.'
Teacher (*smiling at the speaker*): 'Is it possible that we learn more through our failures than through being successful?'

Function: To see this casual and rather dismissive remark as a direct route to the focus of the lesson (without comment).

4. Universalizing the answer

Another way of responding to the casual remark above would be to help students see things in a wider context. The statement, 'There always have to be people who risk failure in order for progress to be assured', could be seen to reflect:
  (a) the wider context of history: Scott is one with all those throughout history who have tried and failed.
  (b) the wider context of the need to be challenged: Scott is one with all those who are prepared to dare.
  (c) the wider context of the competitive spirit: Scott is one with all those who want to be first.

5. Dealing with a student response which downgrades another student's contribution

There are a number of ways of dealing with this kind of remark:
  Student: 'Aw! That's stupid!'
  Teacher:
  (a) 'So far, it's the only idea we have.'
Function: To give acknowledgement to the contribution, implying that others should try contributing.

  (b) 'Perhaps, but do you have a better idea?'
Function: To remind students of the rules of brainstorming.

  (c) 'Hold it! We're just brainstorming here!'
Function: A more overt reminder of brainstorming.

  (d) 'Just a moment! Do we really understand what he said?'
Function: To show the student who has made what was considered by the class as a 'stupid' remark, that the teacher is prepared to consider it.

  (e) 'I am prepared to listen to all ideas.'
Function: To encourage the students to put forward more ideas.

If a remark is truly stupid it will be due to thoughtlessness, inattention, or the desire to disrupt, and should be dealt with accordingly. 'We generally do it with a look, or "I think he forgot where he was", or "Doesn't seem to make sense, does it?" and move on' (Morgan and Saxton, 1987: 90).

6. Giving opportunities for rethinking and restating

'You still think that?' or
'You've changed your mind?'
Function: There are times when students need the opportunity to reconsider their original responses. Or, more directly:
'What made you change your mind?'
'How does that fit with what you were saying earlier?'
Function: In discourse students are often swayed by the views of others and it is important for them to be aware that they *have* changed their views and, more important, that they are able to describe what made them change. This question also helps the student to test out his new view of the situation or idea.

The next part of the chapter deals with specific questioning techniques.

DISTRIBUTION (ALSO REFERRED TO AS 'TARGETING')

This term refers to the way in which questions are directed.
(a) Questions can be directed at an individual, for example:
'John, what have you discovered that we need to know?'
Function: Here everyone but John can relax.

Another way of directing at an individual can generate a momentary tension for the class:
'What have you discovered that we need to know. . . John?'
Function: Here everyone is thinking and assessing but can relax when John is given the responsibility for answering.

(b) Questions can be directed to a particular group:
'What have you *boys* discovered that we need to know?'
Function: The rest of the boys and all the girls can relax.

(c) Questions can be directed at the whole group:
'What have you discovered that we need to know?'
Function: Everyone is thinking and assessing and then may contribute.

There is nothing wrong with directing a question at an individual or a small group as long as you have a specific reason for so doing. Perhaps you are aware that John has something of value from which we could all benefit or you may have seen, as you asked the question, that John wants to answer it. It may be that you have noticed that John is nodding off and needs a wake-up call or you may know that this particular group of boys needs each other's support as they answer.

The reason why 'targeting' has acquired a bad name (apart from its unhappy associations with shooting) is that it is so often used as:

(a) a control ('You're fooling around; pay attention by contributing!');
(b) a means of showing up the lazy or the stupid or the ones who know 'everything'; or
(c) a means of ensuring that everyone on the class list answers a question in turn.

We experienced teachers who did the latter and it was most relaxing until they came to two names ahead of ours, at which time it was advisable to sit up and take notice!

There are other problems with the ways in which teachers distribute questions:

- Some teachers tend to ask more questions of boys than girls (and *vice versa*).
- Some teachers give more questions to high achievers.
- Some teachers give more questions to low achievers.
- Some teachers 'target' specific kinds of questions to specific kinds of students (complex and abstract questions to the 'high' academic students and simple, factual ones to the academically less able).
- Some teachers have a tendency to focus their questions to the right side of the class (or to the left); some work a 'fan'; some work the triangle; some the front rows, some the middle, some the back rows. Students soon learn to gravitate to the 'hot spot' if they want to be noticed and to the 'cold spots' if they haven't done their homework, are tired, bored or need to complete an assignment for the next class.

You need to be aware of your own particular questioning distribution patterns in order to (like the stand-up comic or the club singer) 'work the room'. The keys for unlocking general participation are to:

- support the weak;
- encourage the triers;
- tolerate (and see the potential for learning from) contrary opinions; and
- appreciate the contributions made by your bright students, as aids to your own teaching process.

REINFORCEMENT

Other words for 'reinforce' are 'fuel', 'brace' (as in 'strengthen'), 'succour' or 'nourish'. The effect of this technique is to give students a feeling of success, a feeling that they 'are on the right track' which, in turn, gives them the sense that they have some control, some voice in directing their own learning. It is a most effective way of encouraging participation. Different students respond to different kinds of reinforcement and there are many ways of supporting students and their work.

1. Verbal reinforcement

Such words or phrases as 'good', 'well done', 'that's interesting', 'good point' and so on, confirm for the student that his contribution is not just accepted but that it is approved.

Another means, probably the most powerful of all, is to use the students' words and ideas within your own 'teacher text':

> Student: 'Surely they could have found better ways of using their money than wasting it on badly planned exploration to a place no one is ever going to?'
> Teacher: 'I wonder how much money we've "wasted on badly planned" space explorations?' (using the words), or
> Teacher: 'I wonder if we could say the same thing about our space explorations?' (using the ideas).

Reinforcing is a powerful tool for encouraging participation but, used dishonestly as praise for poor work, it loses its effectiveness. How then, can you acknowledge contributions which are sincere but 'off track' or incomprehensible? Some useful phrases are:

- 'Thanks for that answer.'
- 'Remember our focus is. . . . Can we tackle this answer again, keeping this in mind?'
- 'Yes, those ideas may be useful to us later on.'
- 'Uh, huh. I hadn't thought of that.'
- 'Yes. I'm not sure that we share enough of your reference points to take your meaning.'

A word of warning: Don't fall into the habit of using reinforcing words or phrases as a means to fill in thinking time, either for yourself or while you are waiting for a response from someone else.

2. Minimal encouragements

These are audible prompts which indicate that either the teacher is interested in what is being said or that the student is to continue: 'Hmmmm', 'Ummmm', 'Uh, huh', 'So. . .?', 'Then. . .?', 'Yes. . .?' 'I see . . . '.

3. Non-verbal reinforcements

The body itself is the most direct communicator of messages. Non-verbal signalling (also referred to as 'body language') can be a powerful means of both asking questions and reinforcing answers and it can be a more direct and less threatening means of querying a contribution. You 'signal' your involvement with your students by the way in which you make, hold, break or lose eye contact; you 'signal' your intellectual and emotional engagement by your facial expressions and your body position.

(a) Eye contact

The eyes are the 'window of the soul'. Eye contact is not about being 'eyeball to eyeball' (which can be extremely threatening and inhibiting) but about being able to see how students are connecting with you and how you are connecting with them.

(b) Facial expression

We read reaction through facial expression: the raised eyebrow (could mean, 'I don't understand'), the frown (could mean, 'This is interesting' or 'What are you trying to tell me?'), the closed eye(s) (conspiracy/deep thought/consideration), the smile ('You're doing well, keep going'). There are, of course, negative reinforcements such as the curled lip, the flared nostril, the rolling eyes, all signals that what is being contributed is being received, judged and found wanting!

(c) Body gestures

Some examples of body gestures are: nodding the head ('That's right, keep going'), shaking the head ('Amazing! What will you think of next?'), finger-pointing for emphasis, to isolate a place or focus on a student, shaking the finger ('Stop that! Let's get on'), shrugging the shoulders ('Who cares?', 'Is that important?'), the still look and the silent scan ('Do you all agree with that?', 'Are you ready?').

(d) Body positions

Where you stand or sit in relation to your students and when, how and where you choose to move can be strong indications of your willingness to control or to hand over control. The actual shape of your body (leaning forward in your chair, leaning back against the wall) and what you are doing with your arms, hands, legs and feet (arms folded, twiddling fingers, swinging legs, tapping feet, etc.) all send significant signals which can promote and encourage, or inhibit and discourage engagement.

Eye contact, expression, gesture and position are not actions which can be planned but are your body's natural responses to your thinking and feeling. Non-verbal signalling is the primary message that your students read and therefore it is imperative to be as aware of what you do and how you do it as of what you say and how you say it. The silent language and the audible language must be congruent if they are to register the kind of reinforcement you intend.

PROBING

Probing is a technique designed to help students to think out answers more thoroughly, to encourage quantity and quality of participation, to require students to be more accurate and specific. Some useful 'probing' questions are:

'Can you be more specific?'
'What makes you think that?'
'What about the other side?'
'How might other people see this?'

For example, students often have difficulty in finding the words to describe an abstract concept and so answer with concrete examples. The teacher can use their concrete ideas as a base from which to build into the abstract.

Teacher: 'What is nationalism?'
Student A: 'Flags.'
Student B: 'The national anthem.'
Students: (silence)

The teacher hopes for more but nothing more is forthcoming. It is at this point that she need to use 'the probe'.

'That could be an interesting way of looking at it. . . . '
Function: She is acknowledging and suggesting that there are other ways but giving no help to find them.

But, alas, one is more likely to hear the following, and we include them so that you may recognize them when you find yourself doing just this:

'Come on. What else?'

If they had known 'what else', they would have said.

'That isn't what I asked.'

Nothing has changed except that by criticizing she has probably closed down the discourse.

Had the teacher accepted the student responses of 'flags' and 'anthems' and begun her probe at this concrete level, she might have been able to lead them into the abstract in this way:

Teacher: 'Where have you seen a flag flying?'
Student: 'Outside the school.'
Teacher: 'How many of you notice the flag when you come into school in the morning?'
Students: (a show of hands)
Teacher: 'I wonder why a national symbol flies over our school?'
Student: 'To show that this is a "Canadian" school.'
Teacher: 'Of what sorts of things does our flag remind us?'
Student A: 'That we are all Canadians.'
Student B: 'We are under the protection of Canada.'
Student A: 'At the Olympics it told the world that we were the host country.'
Student C: 'When we discover a new place, we put the flag there to show that we were first.'

Function: Using the probe, the teacher is able to help her students state their ideas. From these they are able to arrive at a definition of nationalism.

The 'counselling' probe

There are times when a student's personal experience is influencing his performance and a teacher will need to work with this student on an individual basis. We are not suggesting replacing the work of counsellors or psychologists, but using the probing technique may help the student to understand more clearly through helping him to reflect on the problem.

Student: 'Everyone in my group thinks I'm stupid.'
Teacher: 'Who, specifically, thinks you're stupid?'
Student: 'I know Mary does.'
Teacher: 'How does Mary show that she thinks you're stupid?'
Student: 'I just can't work with her.'
Teacher: 'What stops you from working with her?'
Student: 'She never listens to my ideas.'
Teacher: 'Can you say "I never listen to her ideas"?'
(And so on . . .)

Using the probe in this way (reflecting the student's own words at an unhurried pace) can help him to look at an academic or personal problem. It is also a useful technique for analysing a group process and the student's part in it. In all cases, the teacher's stance must be one of non-judgemental *active* listening and her responses need to be 'lean, concrete and relevant' (Roth, n.d.). The key words in the questions are Who? What? When? Where? and How? but *never* Why? The task is to help the student to make meaning for himself and not to interrogate him.

WHEN *NOT* TO ASK A QUESTION

It is possible that by now you have decided that the only way to teach is through questions, but there are times when it is not appropriate to ask questions:

- When the students have insufficient knowlege and experience from which to draw an answer: all students can do in this case is to share their ignorance, often reinforcing wrong information and allowing the expression of uninformed and ill-informed opinions. This is a time when students should be encouraged to *ask* questions, not answer them.

- When students are working things out for themselves and progress is being made: you don't want to intrude on productive work however much you may know the right question to ask to put them into the solution! It is often a temptation to use a question as a means of entering a group discussion. Two favourite questions are: 'Are there any problems?' and 'How are you all getting along?' These are maddening interruptions which ask a group to move backwards into review just as they are moving ahead! It is better to sit on the fringe and listen. You will soon discover where they are and what difficulties they are having.

- Often, when we see a student who seems to be having problems, our first instinct is to ask a question because we naturally are concerned and perplexed. We have a terrible tendency to say something like, 'Now, Chris, what seems to be the problem?' or 'Are you all right?' It is much better to use a gentle statement such as, 'You are very quiet today' and then become an active listener, allowing Chris to do the talking if he wants to talk about it. In this way he knows that you are aware and interested in him without demanding an answer which, possibly, he cannot articulate or which he may not want to articulate at the time.

Having taken these points into account, it is now time to look at what happens after you have asked a good question.

DEALING WITH ANSWERS

The process of inquiry does not stop after the question is asked and the answer is given. Like a rally in a game of tennis, the ideas go back and forth for as long as they are able to be sustained. Being able to sustain the rally and send the ball back is as much a part of questioning technique as being able to put the ball across the net in the first place. The way in which you handle this part of the process will become a model for your students.

Let's examine one question and answer exchange and the kinds of responses it can generate.

Teacher: 'Knowing the sort of hardship that would be experienced on the Scott expedition, what qualities would you look for in your team?'

Student: 'They would have to be strong.'

This is a perfectly acceptable answer and there are many ways of responding to it:

(a) By acknowledging the answer with a look or gesture and waiting.
Function: To indicate that the teacher is waiting for further suggestions.

(b) 'Ye.. e.. es.'
Function: Acknowledging the answer verbally and waiting for further answers.

(c) 'Yes, that is a useful quality.'
Function: Acknowledging and reinforcing the contribution. Still open for further suggestions.

(d) 'Yes, that's a useful physical quality.'
Function: Accepting the contribution but, by focusing on the 'physical', the teacher is suggesting that there are other aspects of 'quality'.

(e) 'What kind of strength are you talking about?'
Function: Accepting the contribution but pressing the student to define what he means by 'strong' in order to build common knowledge.

(f) 'What kind of strength is Glen talking about?'
Function: Accepting Glen's idea as a stimulus for analysis by the class.

(g) 'Yes, you would have to be strong: physically, mentally and spiritually.'
Function: Accepting the student's words and idea and extending the concept because: the teacher wants to move on quickly; Glen doesn't often contribute and she wants to make his contribution significant; or this class is not capable of seeing strength in anything other than physical terms and the teacher uses this opportunity to offer some abstract concepts.

(h) 'If all our team are strong, will we need to look for experience?'
Function: Accepting contribution but pressing the class to look for implications ('We can pull the sleds but what if we don't know how to pack them?').

(i) 'Yes, the weak, the handicapped, the Stephen Hawkins of the world can never experience this kind of frontier exploration.'
Function: Accepting the idea and regretting the implications of it, thus allowing students opportunities to rethink.

There are times when we hear an answer that we instinctively assess as 'superficial' or, perhaps, 'typical' of our class. Suppose the student answered the question, 'What qualities would you look for in your team?' by saying, 'They'd all have to be rich.' The teacher might respond by saying:

'All you kids think about is money' or
'I asked about *quality*' or
'I suppose you'd be thrilled to have a rock star on your team.'

Function: Here we can see that the teacher has heard only 'money' which is the standard by which these students measure everything and she is reacting from her own emotional bias instead of hearing the truth of this reply: money *is* important in this kind of venture. Her response could better have been:

'Yes, these expeditions are expensive and the kinds of human qualities the team possesses will be very important if we don't want to waste the money.'

Function: To accept what is given and elevate the thinking.

The teacher can then either leave silence for them to think again about the question she has asked previously or she may want to define what is meant by 'qualities'.

You will notice that when you deal with answers by responding to the ideas within the answer, you are following more closely the rules of 'normal' conversation rather than evaluating the answer and asking another question as in *'recitation'*, for example:

'Good, Glen. Mary, what quality would you suggest? O.K. Nathan, what about you? Nathan, have you been listening? Pia. You usually have some interesting ideas . . .? (And so on. . . .)

Wrong answers and no answers

Susan Dressel (1981) did an interesting study in which she looked at student answers which appeared, to the teacher, to be wrong. Dressel discovered that, in many cases, the student's answer was right according to the 'reference base' he was employing. In other words, we construct meaning out of the frames of reference we already have and when those don't relate to the teacher's it can be extremely frustrating. She suggests that it is important for both teachers and students to 'consciously discuss and identify their own and each other's reference bases' by asking a question like, 'How do you know?' or saying, 'Show me what you mean.' Answers that appear to come 'out of thin air' or 'off the wall' are coming from somewhere; a gentle 'What makes you think that?' can be very revealing and often very useful.

If you are aware that your reponse has indicated to the student that his answer is either wrong or weak, you should try to return later with a question which will allow him to answer more positively.

'Now that you have had time to listen to the others, what ideas do you have about all this?'

Function: To enable the student to have an opportunity to be successful and to let him know that one wrong answer does not 'make a summer'!

Suppose you ask a question to which students cannot find an answer? It is important to let them understand that it is alright for them not to know. 'I don't know', 'I don't know what you mean' or 'Could you say that another way?' or simply silence are not challenges to the teacher, indications of student stupidity or evidence of teacher failure. They are valid responses by students (and even by teachers) and have their place in classroom discourse or discussion just as they do in everyday conversation.

Any teacher response to a student answer will depend upon the class, the focus of the lesson activity or the lesson and the kind of thinking and engagement the teacher wants and/or the students need. Acknowledgement, recognition and the way in which you respond to student contributions are powerful means of generating classroom discourse.

RESPONDING TO ANSWERS: SOME THINGS TO TRY TO AVOID

This section may appear to be repeating what has already been said but it demonstrates a number of common reactions that teachers have, often unintentionally and with the best interests of the students at heart. We suggest you try to:

1. Avoid manipulating responses by non-verbal signals

Students are great sign readers and generally like to please. They can (and do) change answers in response to the signals you are sending by your:

- facial expressions: The frown which can be read as 'Do you know what you are saying?'; the smile which can be read as 'Not bad for a dumb kid!'.
- gestures: The finger snap which can be read as 'Hurry up!'; the dismissive turn of the head which can be read as 'I wish you weren't in my class'.
- non-verbal utterances: The sigh in 'Yes, Kirk' which can be read as 'I never expect a right answer from you'; the in-drawn breath which can be read as 'What nonsense!'.

These kinds of expressions have more power to discourage, antagonize, mock and patronize than any words that you may choose to say and, in reading these messages, students may attempt to adjust their answers (and their behaviour) in order to restore their comfort level.

2. Avoid verbal responses which are detrimental to learning

- Sarcasm: 'Well, we do seem to know a lot about Scott, don't we?'
- Vague and ambiguous statements: 'Oh, I suppose that answer is close enough.'
- Leaping to *your* conclusion:

  Student: 'They should have eaten the dogs.'
  Teacher: 'So you believe in vivisection?'

3. Avoid 'Yes, but. . .' and 'Yes, and . . .'

You can, inadvertently, put yourself back into a control position by responding to a student's contribution by using either of these:

Student: 'I think if I'd been Scott's son I would have resented that he threw away his life.'
Teacher: (a)   'Yes, but surely you would have enjoyed being the son of a hero?' or
            (b)   'Yes, and he might have lived to do something worthwhile.'

In both these replies the teacher has taken the initiative away from the students. In (a) there is an unspoken criticism in the teacher's follow-up which, although a question, does not really invite an answer. In (b) the teacher has taken over the student's idea by completing his thought herself. Much better to remember the lesson focus and acknowledge the remark/ answer and wait to see if other students have anything to contribute.

4. Avoid reacting to every contribution

Reacting to every student contribution with some kind of verbal response such as 'Good', 'Right', 'Well done', refocuses the attention onto the teacher and inhibits student-to-student interaction. Nothing can be more detrimental to discourse than, after every response, to have every student looking to the teacher for an evaluation. Your attitude of interest and attention will be sufficient.

5. Avoid reinforcing prejudices

Student: 'If there'd been black explorers, they wouldn't have got lost in the blizzard' (laughter).

Remarks such as this can offer opportunities for learning, however, there is a tendency for teachers to over-react:

'And what do you mean by that, Jeff?'
Function: Upgrading a remark that is not worthy of that kind of attention.

'I won't have those remarks in my class. Go to the office!'
Function: The teacher is again giving more status to the remark than it deserves and passing the buck to the Vice-Principal.

'And you, Jeff, would easily be found in a dark jungle.'
Function: The teacher is playing Jeff's game and by so doing is suggesting that jokes about colour are acceptable.

Some suggestions for dealing with remarks of this sort:
'Jeff, whatever you mean by that, it's not worthy of you. Janet. . . . '
Function: The teacher acknowledges that she has heard and does not approve and moves on.

Or:
'Matthew Henson explored in the Arctic. It's only now that we are recognizing his contributions. He was black. Janet. . . .?'
Function: The teacher de-fuses Jeff and diffuses the remark by giving out new and interesting information and moves on.

Or:
'Janet, why do you think it took so long to find them?'
Function: The teacher ignores the remark and moves on, thereby implying that the remark was not appropriate and Jeff should know it.

6. Avoid asking questions to which students cannot possibly know the answer

For example:
'What do you think I've got in store for you today?' or
'I wonder what I would have done if I'd been Captain Scott, Mary?'
Oh, dear! We have heard these kinds of questions defended as being 'creative'. Indeed!

7. Avoid asking for choral answers

This is especially true for some elementary classrooms.
'Captain Scott was a hero. All heroes are great men. Therefore, Captain Scott was a. . . . (altogether now). . .?'
Choral answers are a technique of rote learning. This book is not about rote learning!

8. Avoid answering your own question!

'What was the reaction in England when they heard of Scott's death? Naturally, they would have been very proud of his achievement ... deeply sorry for his young family ... disappointed that he wasn't first...?' It takes a confident student to reply, 'You've already answered your own question!' Nothing is more frustrating for a student than having a teacher do this just as he has thought up what he considers to be a really 'good' answer.

9. Avoid counter-questioning

Teachers think that students learn through questions. They do. These questions do not, however, need to be asked only by the teacher and when a student asks a question try not to 'play back' with one of your own.

Student: 'What kind of dogs did Scott take to the Pole?'

Teacher: 'What breed do you think would suit those conditions?'

Student: 'I don't know.' (He wants to add, 'That's why I asked you.')

Dillon (1983: 37) cites research that found that elementary teachers counter-question two of every three student questions. 'A counter-question says, "I'm the one that asks the questions around here."' Rather than countering, the teacher could ask the rest of the class if anyone has the information; she could answer the question herself, if she knows or she could ask someone to find out the answer.

10. Avoid asking questions that have already been answered

In the talk following the question, 'What preparations were made for the journey?', the students discussed at some length the kinds of food that would not spoil when frozen. The teacher then asked, 'What kind of food did they carry with them?' What she is signalling is that she was not listening to the discussion, only waiting to ask the next question on her plan.

11. Avoid asking another question before the students have had time to contribute their answers

When you 'fire' questions at your class, it promotes a pattern suggesting that questions can only have one, perhaps two answers.

Teacher: 'What kind of man was Oates?'

Student: 'He was a romantic.'

Teacher: 'Would you say that of his companions?'

We have lost twenty-nine other possible contributions to the character of Captain Oates.

12. Avoid redirecting a 'right-answer' question

Research demonstrates that this kind of redirection gives the impression to students that the first answer received was incorrect.

Teacher: 'What is Scott's first name, Arthur?'
Arthur (promptly): 'Robert.'
Teacher: 'Mary . . .?'
Mary: (. . . pause . . .) 'Well . . . (thinks: "I'm sure Art was right . . ."). . . (thinks again). . . . '
Teacher: 'Joan. What was Scott's first name?'
Joan: (thinks: "Mary's usually right . . . she doesn't know . . .")
She shrugs.
Teacher: 'Paul . . .?'
Paul (who is bright enough to be bored by this foolish exploration and is doodling in his textbook, looks up and says): 'Robert.'
More has been lost here than time!

13. Avoid collecting answers until you get the one you want:

Teacher: 'What other events in modern times would be analogous with Scott's expedition?'
Student: 'The Canadian attempt on Everest?'
Teacher: 'Y. . .es.'
Student: 'People who try to get to the North Pole by motorcycle, or on skis, or whatever . . . '
Student: 'Carl Lewis . . . Steve Bauer?'
Student: 'Lots of athletes don't come first.'
Student: 'Didn't the Russians try to get to the moon, too?'
Teacher (enthusiastically): 'Y . . . ES!'
Student: 'What about the Challenger?'
Teacher: 'RIGHT!'

There are a lot of good answers here which might have developed new perspectives on the teacher's focus but, alas, she was looking to her students to confirm her own thinking.

14. Avoid phrasing the question for the answer you want

For example:
'You wouldn't want to do that, would you?';
'I don't think that would work, do you?';
'Surely you don't think that?'
Who would be foolish enough to disagree?

15. Avoid hearing only what you want to hear

Teachers must be careful not to hear only what they want to hear. Students will see the teacher as having a listening problem if what happens after they have contributed doesn't fit into the logic of their thinking and the dialogue and so they may give up contributing. These kinds of thoughts may be going on in their minds:

'This isn't the way she wants it to go.'

'What does she want?'

'Why can't she hear what I am *not* saying?'

'Why doesn't she just get on and teach us what she wants us to know and stop asking these questions?'

16. Avoid insincere praise

Using praise as a means of 'jollying' the students along when the quality of their work does not merit it ('Good try, Emily' when Emily has obviously not tried at all) destroys the questioning process. Undeserved praise will quickly put an end to any attempts at critical thinking, clarity and accuracy. Students resent praise when they know they haven't earned it because it makes earned praise worthless. Reserve your praise until it is justified.

17. Avoid asking questions too soon

Sometimes students have been involved in an experience at a deeply personal level. Expecting them to talk about it before it has had time to 'settle', will be not only unproductive but it can destroy or trivialize the experience for them.

18. Avoid asking questions when students are too tired to think

Despite the fact that 'nothing appears to be happening', thinking is a very demanding activity and it is a useless exercise when students are very tired. It would be more productive to put them into some sort of physical task or have them take a 'cat-nap'.

In this chapter we have looked at general teaching techniques which will help to establish an authentic environment for classroom inquiry. In the next chapter we will look at why it is so important for students to be included as questioners in this process; examine the major impediments to their inclusion and suggest ways of overcoming them.

Question: 'One moment, I have a concern. It would seem that having read 102 pages to develop and improve my questioning skills, you are now suggesting that I withhold my expertise?'

Answer: 'Yes . . . and no.'

Chapter 10

The case for the student as questioner

> I expect very little resistance to the claim that in the development of
> intelligence, nothing can be more 'basic' than learning how to ask productive
> questions.
>
> (Postman, 1979: 140)

No one would deny that we learn more in the first three years of our lives
than in any other similar time period. The process of inquiry starts from the
moment of birth and the acquisition of language is the result of that process
and, at the same time, the tool for that process. Small children, as we know,
are the most persistent of questioners:

'What are you doing?'
'Planting seeds.'
'What are seeds?'
'They grow into flowers.'
'How?'
'Rain and the sun help.'
'Does the rain make me grow?' . . . and so on until the parent says, finally
    and firmly,
'Because.'

At home before attending school, children see themselves as 'partners in
dialogue' with their parents and research demonstrates that they initiate
more than half of the questions asked (Edwards and Westgate, 1987: 170).
They are learning through questions: theirs and those of others with whom
they come in contact. If children do learn through questioning and the
purpose of schools is to further learning, it would seem logical that the ratio
of approximately one adult question to one child question would be
maintained throughout the child's schooling.

In a time of working mothers and single parent families, opportunities
for conversational partnerships for the young child would appear to be
greatly reduced. Where one would expect the 'linguistically-rich'
environment of a nursery school to make up for the 'language-deprived'
home environment, it has been discovered that most homes still provide
better opportunities than the schools for learning through talk with an
adult. In the Tizard and Hughes investigation (1984), those children asking
more than 50 per cent of questions at home were asking *under 5 per cent* of
the questions in their nursery schools! Research shows very little increase

in students taking greater responsibility for questioning in their schooling, and a multidisciplinary study on *Questions and Discussion* (Dillon *et al.*, 1988a) revealed that, in the senior grades, students were still asking less than 15 per cent of the questions (Bridges, 1988: 26).

Question: If questioning is a powerful way to learn as well as to teach, why are there not more questions coming from students?

Answer: There seem to be five main reasons for this

---

1 The pressure that is placed upon teachers by parents and school administrators to demonstrate that students possess the knowledge to enable them to gain high marks – 'right-answer' pressure.
2 The pressure that teachers place upon themselves to cover the curriculum.
3 The pressure placed upon teachers by 'external' examinations.
4 The pressure that arises from conventional classroom arrangements that appears to require teachers to conform to traditional teaching methods.
5 The pressure on the teacher to be seen by colleagues, administrators and the students as 'in control' – of herself, her students and her subject.

These are five realities and we are not so out of touch with reality as to suggest that teachers ignore parents and administration, forget about exams, throw out the curricula, risk dismissal and make life miserable for their students and their colleagues. But even taking all these pressures into consideration, if we accept that children are natural questioners and that they learn by questioning, and if we are in the business of 'learning', then it would seem imperative that we make room in our teaching for our students to capitalize on their natural ability to question.

HOW?

A study by Good *et al.* (1987) indicates that if the environment is appropriate and the adults in the environment are open, knowledgeable and supportive, those systemic conditions mentioned above can be overcome. We offer some suggestions.

Right-answer pressure

Tests and exams deal mainly with objective knowledge, known facts and information. Therefore, the questions that are asked are ones to which there is, most often, a right answer; Egan (1987) goes so far as to suggest that test questions examine only the most 'superficial' level of understanding. If a teacher teaches only to this agenda there is no place for the kinds of questions that stimulate a variety of possible answers and generate thoughtful questions in return. Let's look at how two teachers might handle this matter. In a unit on Environmental Studies, the following were test questions:

1 Describe the qualities of Freon gas.
2 What is the effect of Freon gas on the ozone layer?
3 How important is the ozone layer to world environments?

Teacher A teaches the definitions of Freon gas and the ozone layer and describes the importance of the ozone layer. The right answers to the test questions demonstrate the effectiveness of her teaching of the facts and the students' ability to listen, store and retrieve the facts.

Teacher B assigns reading on the material and asks the class to consider, while they are reading, something the teacher overheard in the supermarket, 'After suffering through last winter, the world can't warm up too soon for me!' Class time is given over to discussion on this statement, during which the teacher's educational focus is to ensure that the test questions cited above can be answered. Her role in the discussion group is to offer support, opposition, alternatives and information as the need arises.

Teacher A will know from test results that the students know (or do not know) what they need to know. Teacher B will know from the discussion that students know (or do not know) the answers to the three questions. She will know as well, what her students think and feel about that knowledge.

Teacher A asks three questions and her students none.

Teacher B makes a declarative statement and most of the questions come from the students during discussion and are, in the main, asked of each other.

Teacher A spends 30 minutes teaching to the above questions.

Teacher B spends 30 minutes learning what her students know (some of which is not in the assigned reading), learning about her students and, incidentally, learning what her students know and she does not.

We are not suggesting that Teacher A is not a competent teacher nor that is not important to know when to teach this way. What we are suggesting is that there are other ways of evaluating what students are learning and that it is more likely that they will retain that which they have found out for themselves.

Curriculum pressure

Where knowledge is cumulative there is a responsibility to colleagues to make sure that students are equipped with the prerequisite information when they move on to the next grade level. With this kind of responsibility, teachers feel that they cannot 'waste time' with activities which appear to be peripheral to the content.

'What is it that we want our students to learn?' is one of the fundamental questions that faces teachers (Radwanski, 1987: 10).

If, as McGovern (Holt, 1988: ix) suggests, '[t]he schools at best can cover only a tiny fraction of human knowledge and experience', then you are going to have to ask what content your students can *not* do without.

Curriculum guides make the first selection by offering a survey of the material from which teachers can develop their individual courses of study. The next selector is you, the classroom teacher: you decide in discussion with your colleagues upon which areas you will focus. For example, will you and your students explore medieval history through its wars? its economic development? its religious conflicts? or will you see the medieval world through the eyes of a small village? (Social Studies Curriculum Guide, 1988: 14–33). You make your choice on the basis of your personal preferences and upon your students' frames of reference. Whatever choice you make will, of course, include all aspects of the area of study (economy, conflicts, social organization and so on), as they affect your focus. Can you see, then, how the following questions for discussion need not be peripheral to the content?

1 'Are there 'modern day' crusaders?'
2 'I don't suppose our societal structures are any less hierarchical than they were in feudal times?'
3 'Under what circumstances would a community today feel the need to isolate itself?'

How you teach is entirely dependent upon your answer to the question, *What is it you want your students to learn?* If your answer is that students must become manipulators and questioners, as well as receivers of knowledge, it will be possible for you to find opportunities for students to question within your course time allocations. As one teacher put it, 'We should be in the business of helping our students to *uncover*, not to cover, the curriculum.'

External examination pressure

The need for external examinations are the result of political will. Their purpose is to discover what students have been taught.

Institutions of higher education want an objective yardstick to measure their 'intake'; administrators are interested in the reputation of their schools; parents and students want 'high marks' which will guarantee entrance to the next level of education. Classroom teachers are, themselves, aware that they, too, are being examined and are concerned that students' poor results may affect their positions.

External examination questions differ from the kinds of questions we have been suggesting. They have to be carefully considered so that the answers can become part of a marking scheme that is as equitable for the student in Vanderhoof as it is for the student in Vancouver. The thrust then, is towards those questions which are fact- and information-based. Where these questions invite opinion it would be unwise of a student to offer his own creative and critical-thinking answers unless he was confident that they matched accepted thought. The answer to the question, 'What forces shaped the character of Hamlet?' would not be the time for him to adopt the thesis that Hamlet was homosexual, however well he is able to support that argument.

The most productive way to deal with external examinations is, first of all, to ensure that students understand why you are teaching in this way. Once that is clear, everyone is better able to get on with what has to be done. Some students enjoy the challenge of the competition with its clearly defined parameters. Students who have 'learned how to learn' and are used to cooperative inquiry and classroom discourse seem better able to cope successfully with external exams than those who have only experienced traditional classroom methodology. It is our experience that the former tend to be more adaptable and flexible in their approaches to tasks, whatever they may be.

Students and teachers for the 'examination year' will toe the party line and although we know this has little to do with education, it has a great deal to do with training and practice, which has a value when it is presented to students as a challenge.

Classroom environment pressure

Rows of desks facing the blackboard, the isolation of the teacher from the group, the inflexibility of the furniture do not encourage easy classroom interaction and the authority of the curatorial staff inhibits most teachers from creative interior design! The time and the physical strain required to rearrange a classroom and then to restore it to its traditional arrangement can be seen as hardly justifying the possible learning outcomes.

This can be a problem especially for first-year teachers who don't feel that they can 'make demands'. If you can't move the desks you can move the students: they can turn around and talk to the person behind; they can talk to the person across the aisle; they can sit on their desks to form small conversation groups.

You can arrange to move the class to a more flexible space such as the resource centre or the cafeteria, where the tables lend themselves to group discussion; music and drama rooms offer carpeted floors which facilitate changing group sizes. However, from our experience it is more satisfactory if you can manage in your own classroom; there is a sense of 'home', of security that is psychologically very supportive to classroom discourse. If you have movable furniture you can redesign the room (after consultation with other colleagues who may be using the room and the curatorial staff) or you can train your students to shift the furniture and put it back with minimum confusion.

A changed environment is a learning motivator: it presents opportunities for those students whose learning styles do not fit the traditional classroom model; it changes the position and the status of the teacher, enabling changes in class empowerment; it promotes a different kind of talk and opportunities for peer learning and teaching. Students more readily engage in question and answer exchanges with each other than with their teachers and 'students' responses to fellow students are longer and more complex than responses to the teacher' (Dillon, 1988b: 154). All of which, we believe, more than justifies finding the ways and the means.

The 'control' pressure

A classroom full of student talk is often viewed with the suspicion that the teacher is a poor disciplinarian because, to the outsider, the class appears to be 'out of control'. This is a major problem because it attacks the very foundations of what is teaching and what is a teacher. When the students are talking, the teacher is seen to be *not* in control – to be *not* teaching, the implication being that she isn't earning her money. Students who are used to working with 'authoritarian' teachers who control the subject and ways students think about that subject, often respond in an aggressive or resentful manner when offered empowerment because they feel insecure with the changed 'rules'.

On the other hand, if the students are enjoying their participation and expressing their enjoyment to others, then the course may be seen by other students and teachers as 'mickey mouse', where 'everyone does what he wants' – again, by implication, the teacher is not controlling either students or subject.

Students at all grade levels want the assurance that school is a place for answers because their outside world is so full of questions which don't appear to have answers. They want to see adults as people who can control things. When the teacher asks questions to which she does not know the answers, some students may go home and say, 'Our teacher is stupid; we had to tell her everything!' which tends to reassure neither parents nor students about your competency!

Question: Are there any solutions to this?
Answer: Well, nothing happens overnight but we do have some suggestions:

- You will need to know why you are teaching in this way. You will need to know that you will be able to assess the learning outcomes. It will take time to find the techniques that work for you and your students.

- You have to understand that your students also need time to adjust to a more demanding learning process: they need time to develop the skills of discourse, to develop confidence in their abilities to work in this way and to perceive that this is an interesting way to learn. It is often a long process until you arrive at the point where your students are ready to accept that, without their contributions, the work cannot proceed. Establishing the criteria for a new kind of teaching/learning process is a time of risk for both teacher and students and so the signals have to be clear and the agenda open. Once established, however, a new classroom relationship will develop.

- You will discover that when students are engaged by the content and taking responsibility for their own work, discipline and management problems are minor and those that do occur are often resolved by the students themselves.

- Part of the maturation process is accepting that 'grown-ups' can be wrong, that there are answers but everyone may not know them and that there are some questions for which we have not yet found the answers. The significant part of your job as a teacher is to offer students the means by which they can take control of their lives by equipping them to find the answers *for* themselves and *by* themselves. And to make sure that your students understand that *this* is the purpose of their education.

- Colleagues who are interested in how children learn will be supportive and you must accept that those who teach to a different agenda will probably continue to question your methods.

- You will need to take time to talk to your Principals and Head Teachers about the kind of teaching and learning that you are practising, so that they will know what to look for when they come into (or pass by) your classroom. You will find, as we have, that they are enthusiastic and helpful. Remember, they and their administrators are being made aware daily, through conferences, memos, the media and their political bosses, of the sorts of persons and the kinds of skills that are required for the twenty-first century.

If the 'ability to learn' is identified as 'the premium skill of the future' by the Economic Council of Canada (1987: 31) amongst others, and if students learn through their own questions, then we will have to provide more opportunities than we presently do, for them to participate as questioners.

Question: Remember the question at the end of the last chapter?
Remember our reply?

Answer: Yes, there are times when you must withhold your expertise
but this doesn't mean that you don't need your expertise.

Although children are natural questioners their talents are not necessarily
going to develop without assistance. The musically gifted, the 'natural'
writer, the well-coordinated athlete all thrive in a supportive environment,
exposure to the best in the field, training by enlightened teachers and many
opportunities to practise. In the next chapter we will examine how you can
model 'relevant, appropriate and substantial questions' (Postman and
Weingartner, 1969), deliberately design lessons where students can learn
about this 'neglected language art' and ensure that there are many
opportunities for your students to 'switch places' with you to practise
questioning.

Chapter 11

Switching places: the student as questioner

> Questions breed actions that lead to further questions, and these, in turn, to the boldness of further inquiring acts . . . the living history of man is the story of the questions he has enacted rather than the conclusions he has anchored in science or dogma.
>
> (Kelly, 1963: 12)

Every time you ask a question you are presenting that question as a model to your students and modelling effective questions will help your students to ask better questions themselves (Hunkins, 1974: 77). There are two ways in which you can model: *covertly* – by which students learn by osmosis, and *overtly* – by which you draw attention to what you are modelling by using a 'think-aloud' or 'talk-about' approach demonstrating to your students that you, too, need to consider how to phrase a question and that you appreciate, and are interested in, effective question-making.

COVERT MODELLING

- Your questions will have reason, focus and curiosity and they will, in some way 'hook in' to the students' frames of reference.
- Your questions will be directed at uncovering information, building meaning and considering implications.
- You will, by listening and thinking along with them, let your students experience the excitement and satisfaction that good questions stimulate.
- You will encourage *their* questions so that your students will come to understand that questions belong as much to them as to you.

OVERT MODELLING

Thinking Aloud

'Just a moment. I have to think how best I can put this question.'
Function: Modelling that the arrangements of words are important in making an effective question.

'I need a little time to find the right question to open this up.'
Function: Modelling that any old question does not do!

'I know there is a question here but I'm not sure what it is.'
Function: Modelling that teachers not only don't have answers, but sometimes can't even find the question. This statement also offers an opportunity for the students to suggest a question.

Praising

'That's a question that makes us think!'
Function: Acknowledging a good question.

'I hadn't thought of that question.'
Function: Acknowledging that good questions don't come only from the teacher.

'Hasn't this group's questions revealed some surprises?'
Function: Acknowledging a group's effort to dig deep into an idea.

Encouraging

'Your questions are better and better!'
Function: Acknowledging students' developing skills as questioners.

'I've heard you ask better questions than that.'
Function: Encouraging them to think more deeply and not to slip back.

'Today your questions made me think.'
Function: Encouraging them to see that their questions are helping the teacher to learn.

Reflecting/Analysing

'What was the question that got us going?'
Function: Helping students to think critically about questions.

'Why was that question so interesting to us?'
Function: Analysing the qualities of a question.

'I wonder if there was another way we could have asked that question to get at a more detailed answer?'
Function: Realizing that the form of a question controls the quality of the answer.

Focusing

'The questions we ask are going to be important, so we must make them carefully.'
Function: Drawing attention to how the questions are made.

'As we are only allowed one question, what is it we need to know and how will we phrase the question to get that information?'
Function: Pointing out that one question, well-phrased, is better than twenty indifferent ones

TRAINING AND PRACTICE

Questioning can be taught as a skill component at any level in the language arts curriculum and as a method of learning in whatever subject areas you are teaching. 'Every teacher,' Neil Postman reminds us, 'regardless of level or subject, must be a language educator' (Postman, 1979: 140).

Training is direct: the students learn *about* questioning by practising questioning. James Moffett (1976) writes eloquently about the necessity of teachers understanding that language is only language *when it is being used*. Teachers who instruct students directly as to how and why we question but do not allow them to practise by using that knowledge as they pursue the curriculum are wasting their time and that of their students.

Here are twelve activities which will provide you and your students with opportunities for direct training in asking questions. The first activity is a means of establishing a partnership between you and your students in designing an appropriate environment in which student questioning can flourish.

1. Building the 'rules'

After a few sessions of 'talk', students may realize that they need some guidelines. Rules which dictate behaviour are more likely to be followed when they have been devised by students themselves. Elementary classrooms often have these student-generated guidelines on their walls and we have, more rarely, seen them in secondary schools.

Some that we have noticed are:

Senior

'Keep the bull for the bull sessions!'
'If you haven't got anything to say, don't say it here!'
'Don't hog the floor!' (illustrated)
'Keep your personal vendettas out of the discussion.'
'Don't assume everyone else is a fool but you.'
'Keep to the point!'
'The opinions expressed here are NOT food for gossip there!'

Elementary

> 'If everyone speaks at once, no one can hear anything.'
> 'Speak up, listen hard and take turns.'
> 'THINK before you speak.'
> 'Everybody gets to talk.'
> 'Talk about things that matter.'
> 'WE, in Grade Five, WELCOME YOUR OPINIONS.'

These can be amended as the year goes along.

2. Discovering what questions 'do'

If you want your students to examine the kinds of thinking that the different forms of questions promote, we suggest that you decide with your students on a specific topic or source within which to examine the various forms of questions.

Procedure

1 Students brainstorm (in twos or threes) to make lists of their questions on a chosen topic. At the same time you should build *your* questions as 'back-up' to cover forms of questions which they may not use, so that all three categories will be put into operation.
2 Analyse together the kinds of thinking the questions produce.

EXAMPLE
Topic: Trees
Class: Grade 11 (15/16 years old)
Some examples from the brainstorming:

– What chemical changes in leaves cause them to change colour?
– In Pelham (Ontario) they claim to have the largest maple tree in Canada. How do they know this?
– I wonder why we so often use 'trees' as metaphors?
– How can I prevent the destruction of the rain forests of the world?

By analysing their own questions, students will see how questions can do more than elicit information. Questions can help them to see a topic or source from different perspectives; help them to explore a variety of attitudes through their responses and lead them to new questions.

3. Conducting an inquiry/working scientifically (Brownlie *et al.*, 1988)

Procedure

1 Choose your topic.

2 Make board lists under the following headings:
   What do we know (about the topic)?
   What do we need to know?
   Where can we find the answers?
   Who might help us?

3 Students conduct research in response to those questions (individual, pairs, small groups, etc.)

4 New board headings:
   What have we learned? (which is a new version of question 1)
   What new questions do we have? (which is a new version of question 2)

EXAMPLE
Topic: Honey
Class: Grade 5 (10/11 years old)
What do we know?
   – Honey is made by bees.
   – There are lots of different kinds of honey.
   – It's made from flowers.
   – There is a queen bee, little bees and bumble bees.
   – It's sweet. It's made in a hive. In a comb.
   – It is sometimes runny and sometimes hard.
   (And so on . . . .)

What do we need to know?
   – How is honey made?
   – Why don't bees get sticky?
   – What's the thing about bees and pollen?
   – What do they eat when we take the honey?
   – Is it better for you than sugar?
   – Why is it called a comb?
   – Do killer bees make honey?

Where can we find the answers?
   – The library – look in the catalogue under bees, insects, honey.
   – Books at home.
   – Honey jar.
   – Department of Agriculture – Tim's father works for the government.

- Our classroom dictionary.
- Television – nature programmes.

Who might help us?
- Louise's dad. He's a beekeeper.
- Mr Southern has hives on his property.
- Mr Prothero (the science teacher).
- Our parents.

And after the research was completed:
What have we learned?
- Killer bees are no different from other bees, just more bad-tempered. Ordinary bees don't attack unless disturbed. Killer bees will attack if they feel like it. They are not yet in Canada.
- Louise's dad gave us lots of technical knowledge: how many bees to a hive, how much honey one bee can make, etc.
- Ms Lindley (Home Economics) told us the nutritional value of honey.
- When you take honey out of a hive, you put sugar in for them to eat.
- Now I understand about 'busy as a bee'.

What new questions do we have?
- Why are some people, like Jeff, so allergic to bee stings?
- Was honey here before sugar?
- What will happen when killer bees come to Canada?
- If honey is more nutritious than sugar, doesn't it harm the bees when we take it away?

And so the process goes on.

This procedure works well using letters, diary or journal entries, photographs, pictures, newspaper clippings, maths and science problems and so on, as sources for learning through asking questions.

4. The 'ReQuest' Procedure

This reading strategy was designed by A.V. Manzo (1969) to help students develop an 'active inquiring attitude . . . examine alternatives and originate information' (see also Brownlie et al., 1988: 81–6). The teacher asks two or three students to help her ask the class questions about the story they are reading. At the same time as they ask the question, they identify the kind of question: 'on the line'; 'between the lines'; and 'beyond the lines', which you will remember from Chapter 5.

EXAMPLE
Topic: The story of Little Red Riding Hood
Class: Grade 3 (8/9 years old)

Q. Mary: 'Where did Little Red Riding Hood's grandmother live? On the line question.'
A. Alice: *'That's easy. In a house in the forest. Look at the picture!'*
Q. Jason: 'What rule did L. R. R. break when the wolf spoke to her? Between the lines.'
A. Anne: *'She spoke to a stranger.'*
A. Tom: *'And she told him where she was going.'*
Q. Teacher: 'Beyond the line question. I wonder why her mother didn't go with her?'

After experiencing this kind of overt training, students should be able to ask these kinds of questions to themselves as they read in the Language Arts programme and in all other courses of study.

5. Study Guide Questioning

Using questions is an effective way of recalling blackboard, textbook or lecture material.

Procedure

The student formulates and writes down the questions for which the material, in his notes or textbook, supplies the answers.

Later, in discussion, reviewing or preparing for examinations, the student can discover what he knows (or doesn't know) by means of answering his own questions.

EXAMPLE

Text source:
When the goal is to 'cover' *the* content, efficiency and accuracy in delivery of information become measures of 'effectiveness'. If we ask questions we may have to 'waste' time correcting innacuracies in students' responses. If we permit students to ask questions, we may fail to reach our content goals. Yet students' 'inaccurate' answers to our questions, and their irrelevant questions to us, reveal the true 'effectiveness' of our 'delivery system'.

(Kurfiss, 1989: 2)

Question:
What is the 'content coverage myth' and how does it inhibit learning?

6. Making up test questions

Another way you can train students to recognize the significance of their learning is to empower them with a 'teacher-task': creating test questions. This is not a practice exercise but as part of the reflection on the unit of study. Sometimes the making of the questions can become the test itself.

Procedure

Teacher: 'When we are making up tests, we need to ask questions which draw out the information we know, show that we understand the information, and give us opportunities to express our own ideas and opinions about the information.'

EXAMPLE
Topic: Political systems
Class: Students in Grade 11 (15/16 years old)

After discussion these are the questions they agreed upon:
1 What are the responsibilities of the upper and lower houses in the democratic system?
2 In this country, what conditions might lead to the creation of a totalitarian state?
3 Under what political system would you like to hold office?

The students in small groups spent 30 minutes brainstorming the questions. They spent the remaining 30 minutes in discussing, arguing and defending their choices to the rest of the class. This activity revealed to the teacher their knowledge and understanding of this unit of study, served as review and almost made the test redundant!

7. Twenty Questions

This 'old chestnut' of a party game has educative possibilities for questioning training and practice.

Procedure

One or more students choose a specific article *(the sword that Arthur drew from the stone)*, person *(Mother Teresa)* or place *(the Parthenon)*. The rest of the class are allowed 20 questions, to which the answer must either be 'Yes' or 'No' in order to find the answer. They may, at any time, ask directly 'Is it . . .?' ('Is it Jonas Salk?') but if they have not guessed correctly, that 'No' answer is included as part of the 20 questions they are allowed to make. A maximum of 3 direct 'guesses' is allowed.

The function of this game is to help students to think carefully in order not to waste questions. For example,

'Is it male?'

'No.'

'Is it female?'

is an example of a wasted question. The other function is to help students to narrow the field by asking questions to which a 'Yes' or 'No' answer provides pertinent information upon which they can build.

'Is she an athlete?'

'Yes.'

'Does she play winter sports?'

'No.'

is more effective than asking:

'Does she play soccer?'

'No'

'Does she play basketball?' . . .

The twenty questions 'fly by'!

We have found that groups of six where two students select the topic and four ask questions, offers greater opportunities for students to practise. You can also suggest that your students examine the kinds of questions that are asked on radio and television versions or adaptations of Twenty Questions.

8. Hot-seating

Twenty Questions is about asking 'closed questions'. This must be balanced by giving students opportunities to experience making questions which invite the responders to elaborate and originate.

Procedure

Groups of four (A, B, C, D):

1 A chooses a person from history, literature, current events and reveals his choice.
2 B, C and D's task is to design questions where the focus is on drawing out the respondent's knowledge, experience, imagination and feelings by requiring him to read 'between the lines' and 'beyond the lines'. Information questions may be asked where appropriate.
3 A answers in the first person *as if* he were that person.

Students need time to formulate the 'starter' questions. We find it helps to allow A to 'listen in' as B, C and D are formulating their questions so that he can begin to consider his answers.

EXAMPLE

Student A chooses to be Galileo. These are the starter questions formulated by B, C and D:

1 'In what ways did you change the world?'
2 'If you were alive today where would you like to be and with whom?'
3 'What things in your life do you regret?'

This is an exercise that is used to help actors develop their stage characters by being asked questions by fellow actors which demand that they look more deeply into the meanings behind and beyond the words of the script.

9. Question/Question

This 'game' is played by the protagonists in the opening scene of Tom Stoppard's play *Rosencrantz and Guildenstern are Dead*.

Here students are practising making questions by answering each question with a question.

EXAMPLE

A. 'Are we going together?'
B. *'Do you want me to come with you?'*
A. 'Isn't it necessary for both of us to go?'
B. *'How much do we have to carry?'*
A. 'You don't expect me to help, surely?'
B. *'Have you forgotten I have a bad back?'*
(And so on. . . .)

The 'rule' is that you cannot repeat your partner's question and the guideline is that each question should open up possibilities for your partner (Morgan and Saxton, 1987: 104). Bidwell (1990) uses Question/Question as a way of conducting classroom discussion (see Appendix 2).

10. Answer/Question

Paul Bidwell also suggests that an effective means of testing students' knowledge and understanding is to present them with an answer and ask them to provide the questions.

EXAMPLE

'The following excerpt is from *A Bird in the House* by Margaret Laurence. For what question or questions might this be the answer?'

I went upstairs to my room. Momentarily, I felt a sense of calm, almost of acceptance. Rest beyond the river. I knew now what that meant. It meant Nothing. It meant only silence forever.

Then I lay down on my bed and spent the last of my tears, or what seemed then to be the last. Because, despite what I had said to Noreen, it did matter. It mattered, but there was no help for it.

(Laurence, 1978: 93)

Some questions that were suggested:
In the story what evidence is there for Vanessa's lack of faith?
What does Vanessa say about death?
What evidence do we have that there has been at least one other event which has caused her to cry?
Is there a part of the story of Vanessa which parallels your own experience?

There are many games which use question-asking as a means of entertainment (especially at Christmas) and we suggest that you and your students investigate these sources at the Public Library and game shops to find those which you can adapt for classroom use.

11. Role-playing

Role play offers a different way of questioning curriculum content. For example, we can study *Hamlet* by simply reading the text and answering the teacher's questions or we can build, in role as reporters for *People* magazine, the questions we would need to ask in order to file a 'Bio' story. A different aspect of the story would be revealed if Hamlet were questioned by the students in role as psychiatrists.

Role-playing is not about 'acting out', 'acting like', 'imitating', 'showing' or even 'pretending'. In role-playing all that is required of the participant is to see the world through someone else's eyes and in so doing, to respond as that person would think and feel, expressing attitudes and points of view in response to situations, relationships and problems to be solved.

Students have no difficulty in adapting their language to the role because they are used to adapting their language to their changing roles in life. The style, vocabulary, tone, logic, content and metaphors of language in the home are different from those used with peers. The language of the classroom has its own structure which will change depending upon the content and the teacher, and those students who carry part-time jobs adapt to the particular jargon and style demanded by their employment ('Have a nice day!'). Role play in the classroom can offer an infinite number of opportunities to deepen, enrich and extend language experience by inviting students to explore situations *as if* they were someone else.

For example, the way in which senior students interpret a report and question a 'standing committee on the environment' will be quite different if they are in role as environmentalists from being in role as industrialists or as the unemployed workers. Junior students, given the opportunity to work in role as parents called in to the school to discuss bullying, will ask different kinds of questions from those they would ask as if they were school officials called in to investigate student absenteeism.

'The work here is about a task-oriented situation. All that is required is that the task be done seriously and responsibly as any professional would do it. It is this attention to the task which protects the students from worrying about what they sound or look like' (Morgan and Saxton, 1987: 119).

Procedure

Grouping for role-playing: In role play students can work one on one, one on a small group, a small group on one, one on the whole group or the whole group on one or a small group on a small or a large group and so on. For example:

- Put the class into pairs; one student in role as Hamlet is questioned by the other in role as, say, a reporter or psychiatrist.
- The students work in small groups where three reporters or psychiatrists question one Hamlet; or one reporter or psychiatrist questions three members of the court about Hamlet.
- The students work as a whole group in which one student in role as Fortinbras questions those in the court as to what has been going on; or the citizens of Norway can question Fortinbras about the 'rotten' state of Denmark.

Similarily, in an elementary Social Studies class looking at the opening of the American West (O'Neil and Lambert, 1982):

- The whole group as potential emigrants can question the Government Land Agent (the teacher).
- A reporter (student) can question the group about why they want to go West and what they hope to find when they get there.
- In pairs the one who has decided to go can be questioned by one who is still undecided.
- In small groups a grandchild can question the elders of the family about the journey they took so many years ago.
- A small group of modern-day 'historians' can try to find the true story by questioning a number of individuals who took that journey.

Notice in this last exercise how the present and the past are brought together. In role play you can manipulate time which provides another dimension of experience for your students.

Some roles that promote questioning (Morgan and Saxton, 1987: 84–5)

The Learner: the questioner wants to know.

The Absentee: the questioner is filling in the gaps.

The Researcher: the questioner wants to find out something specific.

The Interviewer: the questioner is building a picture of the person being interviewed.

The Media Reporter: the questioner is working with the particular bias of his employer which dictates the kinds of questions which are asked.

The Policeman: the questioner is looking for facts; the focus is on what is or was.

The Detective: the questioner is looking for clues; the questions are designed to be indirect and divergent as incongruities are sought out.

The Lawyer: the questioner is building a case; the focus is on winning the case.

The Devil's Advocate: the questioner is challenging the argument, statements, the story by taking the opposite point of view.

Working in role provides a safety net which gives students the confidence to express attitudes and points of view which they do not normally hold or may be afraid to express as themselves; it gives them the excitement of challenging their peers and the teacher and, because they are manipulating the material themselves, it gives the added dimension of personal investment in curriculum content.

12. Analysing a tape-recording

One of the most effective means of monitoring the development of questioning skills is to use a tape-recorder. Students enjoy analysing their questions by this method and so can you. Tell your students that you are using the tape recorder to help you improve your teaching. They, and you, will soon forget about it. Simply turn it on at the beginning of class and off at the end. When you have the time, sit down and listen to it. There are all sorts of things for which you can listen. For example:

- How many questions am I asking?
- Am I using all the categories?
- What variety of questions am I asking?
- Which questions get the students to talk?
- What is the quality of their answers?
- How long is the 'thinking time'?
- Are my biases showing?
- Who is doing all the talking?
- How many student questions are there?
- What do I need to work on? Voice? Intonation . . .?
  (And so on . . . .)

It takes a little time to get used to listening analytically to yourself. (Students don't seem to have the same trouble!) If you would prefer, invite a colleague into the classroom. Decide together on a short list of things that he or she will listen for and after the class is over, sit down together and discuss the results. You can do the same for your colleague. We know of a number of teachers who have improved their skills in this way and found it, rather to their surprise, to be a very invigorating, as well as useful, experience.

Switching places with your students and working with them as partners to create an active, cooperative learning environment does not mean that you are abrogating your responsibilities as a teacher. Just as the students are taking on different roles so you, too, are adding the roles of facilitator and enabler. This takes time and practice. You and your students are building a new agenda for teaching and learning through which they will come to see you not just as someone who *holds* answers but also as someone who, like them, is *seeking for* answers.

Our final chapter is a sample lesson in which the educational focus is to provide opportunities for students to consider the making of questions, to pose those questions and to face the challenge of having to deal with the answers their questions have engendered.

Chapter 12

The example lesson: 'Ann Graham'

The format of this lesson, designed by Jonothan Neelands in 1987, is a most effective means of promoting student questioning skills. You will notice that the strategy, a combination of 'Conducting an inquiry' and 'Role-taking', enriches the complexity of the task and deepens the intellectual and emotional engagement of the students. The source he uses has proved to be of great interest to students from grade 7 (12 years old) through post-secondary. Sources appropriate to the interests and experiences of other age groups can function equally well within this format.[1]

CLASS DESCRIPTION

Subject: English.
Class: Grade 11 (15/16 years old)
Type: 30 students (14 boys, 16 girls of mixed ethnic backgrounds)
Number of lessons: 4   Time: 1 hour
Class shows:

    1 Average ability.
    2 Eagerness to work in groups of their own choice.
    3 Resistance to using language, either orally or in written form.
    4 Ability to think creatively when interested and challenged.
    5 Very little experience of role play.

Teacher's objectives: Through the building of a collective story, to provide opportunities for students:

    (a) to ask questions and to listen to questions and answers from their peers;
    (b) to analyse and evaluate the effectiveness of those questions; and
    (c) to write stories based on the information gathered from the questions and answers.

Source:

    In 1872, the body of Ann Graham was found by the road that runs from Ashtown to Moose Creek, as it passes the farm of Samuel Taylor.

Ann, daughter of John, a blacksmith of Ashtown, had left her home some months before. No one spoke of her leaving. No one spoke of her death. No gravestone marks her burial place.

THE LESSON

Day 1

Administration:

(a) Ann Graham's story written on chart paper.
(b) Masking tape, chart paper and felt pens for group work.

Teacher introduction:

'This morning we are going to explore the ways in which people make stories together – to see what happens when we lay our stories alongside other people's. This means that we are all going to watch very carefully so that no one imposes his or her story on the story we are *all* making. Let me be very clear about one thing, the story we make *is* the story. Don't come up to me at the end and say "Yes, but now tell us the *real* story" because the real story is the one we will make. All we have is this fragment.'

The teacher puts up the source on the board. 'Just read it quietly to yourselves.' *(They do.)*

Teacher: 'What do we know from reading this fragment?'

Some answers:

Student A: 'Ann Graham died on the road to Ashtown.'
Student B: 'We don't know she died there. Her body was found there.'
Student A: 'You're right!'
Student C: 'Her father was a blacksmith.'
Student D: 'She must have died under strange circumstances because no one spoke of her death.'
Student E: 'We don't know that; people may not have spoken about it because they lived in a community of deaf and dumb people!'
Student B: 'It doesn't read like that. If it were normal, no one would have written it like that.'
(And so on. . . .)

Teacher: 'We really don't know very much, do we? What questions are beginning to form in your mind?' 'Groups of five, please. Take a sheet of chart paper and one felt pen per group. Appoint a secretary to record your questions. Beware of swamping other people's ideas with your own. We are working out of the facts we have and any logical assumptions which arise from those facts. You have about 5 minutes, so get moving!'

Students work well discussing, arguing about the relevance, the wording and the importance of the questions. The teacher stands aside and reminds them of time passing (which turns out to be nearer 10 minutes than 5!).

The groups convene again. Questions are shared and those approved are written on the board, next to the source.

EXAMPLES

Group A: 'How many months was Ann pregnant?' (This question always turns up at this stage!)

Teacher: ' Be careful! You are imposing your own story. We don't know enough yet to make an assumption like that. Can you word the question another way so that that information could be revealed?'

Group A: 'Was Ann pregnant?'

Group C: 'No, that's still not right. We've got a better one! What was the condition of Ann's health?'

Group D: 'We don't know how old she was. We have, 'How old was Ann at the time of her death?'

Teacher: 'What do you want me to write down?'

Group B: 'Put down the one about her age first and then the one about her health.'

Teacher: 'Are we agreed that both will be useful questions?' (They are.)

They go on until there are 15 questions on the board. All the time the teacher is focusing the students on the way in which the question is phrased. For example:

'Is there another way of putting that so that it will open up rather than close down?'

'Can we write that another way so that it gets at what we want to know more directly? Remember we want to keep the story very open at this point.'

'Try not to follow one line but rather make these questions so that they cover a breadth of "territory".'

(And so on . . .)

Teacher: 'Read the questions carefully. . . . Who might be able to answer them?'

Some answers:

– Ann's father
– Samuel Taylor
– The religious advisor

Someone suggests a hairdresser.

Student: 'No! That isn't right with the period.' (An argument ensues. . . .)

Teacher: 'What I'm hearing is that you want to speak to someone who's in a position to know what's going on in the community.'

The students decide on a 'barber'.

- The barber.
- The doctor.
- Ann's best friend (The teacher rejects a suggestion of 'Ann's lover' as being 'I' writing rather than 'we' writing: 'Remember we are building a *collective* story'.)
- The person who found the body.
- The person who buried her.

As the roles are approved they are listed on the board beside the 15 questions.

The teacher asks the students to think about what has happened today but not to build the story on their own. She reminds them that this is to be a 'collective' story.

Day 2

Administration:

(a) The board questions and roles list have been transcribed onto chart paper and are now pinned up on the board beside the source.
(b) Pencils and paper are ready for 'scribes'.

Student (on entering the classroom): 'Are we going on with Ann Graham?'

Teacher smiles and points to the board.

When the class is settled, she asks them to reread the source, the questions and the list of roles.

Teacher introduction:

'This is going to be a very demanding lesson. We need to deepen our understanding of the events surrounding the death of Ann Graham and for that I am going to invite five volunteers each of whom will take on the responsibility of representing one of the roles we have listed on the board.'

Most students are keen to volunteer. Five are selected and asked to stand apart.

The chairs are arranged in a large circle and the rest of the students sit. 'We need to record the questions that we ask of those who are representing the roles on our board list.' Five more students volunteer to be scribes and collect paper and pencils.

Teacher (to the 'scribes'): 'Mary, you record the questions addressed to George; Al, you write the questions we ask Jane'. (And so on. . . .)

Teacher then places five chairs randomly within the circle, facing in different directions.

Teacher (to the five apart): 'You will come in when you are called and sit on any chair you choose. Once you sit, you are in role. Do not decide amongst you now who will be who, but rather begin to make up your mind as you are coming in to sit down.'

Teacher (to everyone): 'We are ready now to question. We will have to listen carefully to the answers we are given because it is upon those answers that we build our story. Remember these people have *agreed* to speak to us. I know you will treat them with respect.'

Teacher (to the students sitting in the circle): 'Thank you for coming today to try and solve the mystery of Ann Graham's death. We are here to find the truth and we have all signed the form not to publish our findings without permission.' (This suggests a general role to the students which will give them a reason for asking the questions.) The teacher goes on: 'It is important to remember that the event we are investigating happened *10 years ago*. There will, therefore, be things which our guests will not be able to remember, things which they simply do not wish to talk about, and things which they cannot talk about.'

Using a gesture only, the teacher invites someone in the 'apart' group to come forward into the circle and sit down in one of the chairs.

Teacher: 'Thank you for coming. May I ask your name and your relationship to or connection with Ann Graham?'

Student (in role): 'My name is John Graham. I am Ann's father.'

Teacher: 'We know you might find some of our questions distressing and that you may have forgotten some of the details of that time 10 years ago. We will understand if you do not wish to answer all the questions. This is not an inquisition. Who has the first question for Mr Graham?'

The teacher follows the same format with the other four students who choose to take on the roles of Samuel Taylor, the barber, a nun at the convent where Ann attended school and 'the person who buried her'.

While they are being questioned, the students in role are not to interact with one another. When 'Samuel Taylor' makes a derogatory comment about 'John Graham', 'John Graham' turns to say something; the teacher intervenes immediately, 'We are speaking to Mr Taylor'.

There are about ten questions per role although the barber has fewer questions because he tends to 'gossip' more, whereas the nun has more questions because she only answers what is asked of her. Of the 61 questions asked, the teacher makes 6 question interventions: 2 questions are for clarification, 1 question because she is intrigued and needs to know for herself and 3 questions are asked in order to open up the questioning or change the pattern of the asking.

Some examples of student questions:

To Mr Graham: 'What was your relationship with Samuel Taylor?'
A good open question providing a number of pieces of information upon which others build their questions.

To the nun: 'And what was Ann's home life like?'
This question invites the nun to support or oppose what a previous speaker has implied. The nun responds, '*I am not in a position to speak of those things*' which is a more powerful answer than had she answered the question directly.

To the barber: 'What do you think of Samuel Taylor?'
The student who asks this question wants information but the way the question is worded gives the barber licence to be creative with his answer which tells us a great deal about the barber, a little about Taylor and nothing at all about Ann's death. When the students later analyse the questions, the teacher uses this question to demonstrate the importance of phrasing.

To Samuel Taylor: 'We understand from Mr Jackson, the barber, that you
    have a son?'
    'Yes.'
    'What are your ambitions for him?'
This exchange comes late in the interview with Mr Taylor; the first question is asked to check that the information previously given is correct; the second question is the key question which begins to unravel the mystery.

The last student to be questioned is a girl.
Teacher: 'I know we've kept you waiting a long time. Thank you for your
    patience. What is your name?'
    'Mrs Jenkins.'
    'Mrs Jenkins, might I ask your connection with Ann?'
    'I buried her.'
Student (quickly): 'How come a woman is burying the dead?' (Which
    opened up another 'can of worms', so to speak!)

At the end of the questioning in role, the teacher addresses the questioners:
'I expect that now there are other questions in your mind which you would like to ask. These people will remain in role and you may go around and ask them any other questions that you may have. Scribes will now have a chance to ask their own questions.'

The group breaks up, moving around amongst the chairs in the centre of the circle, asking questions or just listening to others asking questions. After about 5 minutes the group returns to the chairs.
Teacher: 'Have you picked up any new information which you think you
    should share with us?'

Quite a lot of interesting things are mentioned, phrased in such ways as:
'I learned that . . . ',
'I don't understand why her. . .',
'Mr Taylor seemed uncomfortable about . . . ',
'I think we should all know that. . . '.

The teacher then asks the students to place all the chairs but one against the walls and to stand by them. She collects the question lists from the five scribes and puts them on her desk. She takes the remaining chair, turns it over and places it on the floor in the middle of the room.

Teacher: 'This chair marks the spot where Ann Graham's body is to be buried. Will those of you we questioned please place yourselves *where* you would be and *how* you would be at the time of Ann's burial.'

They do so while the rest of the class watches as the picture takes shape.

Teacher: 'Look at this picture. If there is anything you don't understand, ask a question.'
A student: 'Bill, why are you standing on that chair?'
Bill: 'I don't think Taylor would be at the burial, but I am standing on my hill, watching.'

Students question until everyone is satisfied (seven questions in all.)

Teacher (to the rest of the class): 'Now it is your turn. As members of Ann's village, take a moment to think where you might be and what you might be doing at the moment of Ann's burial.' (She waits.)
    'Now, you will take your place in the picture one at a time.' (They do, in silence.)
Teacher: 'Just hold that picture for a moment. Close your eyes. The body is now being lowered into the ground. What question is in your mind? I shall come around and place my hand on your shoulder. When you feel my hand say your question aloud.'

Some examples (6 of 26; 4 students passed):
    'What was in Ann's mind the moment she faced death?'
    'Why am I not allowed to toll the bell?'
    'Why didn't I do what I knew I should have done?'
    'She asked for it. What's all the fuss about?'
    'I wonder what the person who killed her is thinking now?'
The final question was 'Why?'

After a silence, the teacher says, 'Just find someone near to you, sit down together and when you feel like it, begin talking about the experience.' (They do. They reflect together for about 10 minutes.)

Homework Assignment

Teacher: 'We have been building a collective story but there are still many questions to be answered. Now it is time for you to write about the story as *you* see it. Hold to the facts that have been established but you are free to create your own version. You may write it as a diary entry, a letter, a short story, a newspaper article, as the summary of a trial. . . in any way that you feel is right for what you want to say and how you want to say it. I expect you to have your first draft ready for next class.'

Day 3

This lesson is a 'composition' lesson, fulfilling the third teaching objective: to provide opportunities for students:
    '(c) to write stories based on the information gathered from the
        questions and answers'.

Students work in pairs or small groups, sharing their stories and working as editors with their partners. None of the students completes the assignment in class time. Their completed writings are later handed in in many forms, indicating their commitment to the task and to the work of the previous lessons. Some assignments were on 'doctored' paper to make the document 'look old'; some were letters (one or two sealed with wax); one was in the form of Samuel Taylor's will; a number were written as diary entries and some as short stories.

Day 4

This lesson addresses the second objective: to provide opportunities for students:
    '(b) to analyse and evaluate the effectiveness of those questions'.

Administration:
    (a) Transcribe the questions asked in the in-role interviews; ten copies of each sheet.
    (b) Chart paper and felt pens.

The students spend the class time analysing the questions that were transcribed during the in-role interviews. There are six groups of five and each group receives the questions from two of the interviews (approximately twenty questions).

Task 1

Working on chart paper, arrange the questions under three headings:
    (a) Those which elicit information.

(b) Those which draw answers which fill in between the facts and make connections.

(c) Those which invite answers which develop the story.

Task 2

Decide if there are questions which could have been better phrased and rephrase them.

The teacher collects the sheets in order to check later to see if there is any need for re-teaching.

Task 3

In light of the work students have just done, create three 'great' questions to be addressed to a 'close relation of Ann's mother'.

These are shared and discussed with another group. Some of the 'really great ones' are presented to the whole group. For example:

'Some say it would have been better if she never been born. How do you see her life and death?'

The whole class then moved into a discussion prompted by the question:

'Why are some questions difficult to answer?'

And, after reading this book, we hope that you will have found some answers.

> Once you have learned to ask questions – relevant and appropriate and substantial questions – you have learned how to learn and no one can keep you from learning whatever you need to know. (Postman and Weingartner, 1969: 23)

Differences between social talk, classroom discourse and discussion

Social Talk	Discourse	Discussion
Definition: Unstructured, informal talk	Informal but with a flexible structure and generally centred around a topic theme. Inconclusive, though points for further investigation are identified	Formally structured exchange of ideas, dependent upon analysis, synthesis and valuing, moving towards a conclusion to provide a platform for further identified investigations.
Time Frame: None	Dictated by timetable and class time	Generally defined as part of lesson plan
Leader: No leader	Teacher as arbitrator, reference point and administrator	Teacher, unless a student is specified
Grouping: Flexible as people come and go, depending upon their interest	No one can leave and no one joins in unless invited. Participants opt in or out, intellectually and emotionally. Large group can subdivide. Teacher moves about	Formal large group or assigned smaller groups. Teacher generally central to the discussion (physically)
Point completion: Rarely completed verbal points, very interrupted	More attention given to completing points, less interruptions, though they are acceptable	Each contributor completes his thoughts unless he is rambling at which point leader can intervene

Social Talk	Discourse	Discussion
Agenda: No agenda is planned and anyone can introduce a topic which lives or dies according to the interest of the participants	Topic can be student- or teacher-initiated and students share major responsibility in organization and control of the interaction. Generally discourse takes the form of generating a context for subject material or reflecting on the work	Topic and procedure set by the teacher at initiation of the discussion. Procedure is controlled by the leader. The discussion is based on a previous subject experience or external stimulus (play, novel, experiment, etc.)

Note: Social talk can move into discussion when someone has specific knowledge in which others are interested. Discourse, too, can move into discussion if the teacher senses an interest and feels the contributions need to be organized in a more formal manner.

ON CONDUCTING DISCUSSION

Ferrara (1981: 71) says that 'discussion . . . is a most difficult and demanding process. It involves people as well as ideas; it is social as well as intellectual and a balance must be maintained between the two. The discussion leader must learn to listen, to question and to enjoy the process itself.' Teachers often see their place in a discussion as the 'asker of questions' but discussion demands an exchange of ideas and so students, too, have a right to express their ideas in the form of questions. The questions that they ask will help the teacher to know what it is they need to learn. The teacher's role in a discussion is that of an 'impartial provocateur who assists the group to engage in the subject as comprehensively as possible' (Ambrosino, n.d.: 18); to put the class at ease, to encourage the talk, to maintain respect for the process, to conclude gracefully and to review immediately. In reviewing, the teacher should note what happened sociologically (who spoke?) and intellectually (what about?).

A MODEL FOR DISCUSSION:

1 Have your question(s) ready. One good question should be enough to generate discussion.
2 Be clear about your expectations and share them with the class.
3 Introduce the topic, develop an outline and try to stick to it (you could use the blackboard).
4 Ask the class for their reactions to the source material in order to generate some common ground and identify individual concerns, relate these to the topic and the outline and, with the agreement of the students, establish the focus.

5 Exploration of the topic: this can appear to be an 'untidy' step as things are being sorted out. There are some specific jobs that the teacher can undertake:

- watch for 'personal storying' or irrelevancies and intervene to refocus,
- keep an eye on the relationship of the variety of ideas to the focus and the outline,
- keep an eye on the passage of time,
- watch for time-consuming and fruitless arguments,
- encourage everyone to participate and to share ideas and experiences,
- deflect those who start to dominate the discussion,
- help students to understand by moving their frames of reference from self to seeing from other perspectives, and
- close off something when it has been sufficiently discussed.

6 Conclude by summing up the flow of the discussion.
7 Invite suggestions for further action and volunteers for further responsibilities.

Note:
Whether a discussion is teacher or student-led, the teacher is responsible for the outcomes. Remember that feelings expressed in discussion are neither right nor wrong, they just *are*. Mutual acceptance of feelings paves the way for accommodation to others' attitudes and points of view.

A REMINDER OF SOME OF THE KINDS OF QUESTIONS THE TEACHER CAN ASK TO SUPPORT AND ENCOURAGE DISCUSSION

1 Questions which focus on the shared experience: What happened? What did we see? What do we now know?
2 Questions which focus on individual contributions: What do you think (name)? What have you discovered? How did you contribute (name)?
3 Questions which focus on meanings arising from the experience: Why did we decide that? What was this really about? Have we discovered anything new about . . .?
4 Questions which focus on projections and hypothesis: What could have happened? What will happen?
5 Questions which focus on making connections: What has this to do with . . .? Does what we now know change anything? Can you see the connection between this and . . .?
6 Questions which focus on future action: What do we need to do next? I wonder what consequences this will have on . . .? How does this affect what will happen next?

7 Questions which focus on personal feelings: What was concerning you when . . .? How did you react to . . .? You seemed to be afraid/worried/ concerned when . . .?
8 Questions which focus on making value judgements: Do you think we were right to . . .? Can you think of a better way to . . .? Would it be/have been more effective to . . .? Can you think of a better way to . . .?

The notes above are based on research by Charles Ferrara (1981), R.E. Lefton, K.R. Buzzotta, M. Shenburg (1980), S. Ambrosino (n.d.), W.J. McGeachie (1978) and John Norman (1987).

Appendix 2

'Quescussion'

The following is an example of Question/Question as it is applied in the work of Paul Bidwell. He sets his students the problem of exploring a source only through questions; should anyone forget to use the interrogative, someone else says 'statement' as a reminder of the rule. We include it as a demonstration of a number of principles which we have described. Notice how the students monitor their own work, focusing and refocusing the 'quescussion', and how they bring what is important and relevant to themselves to bear on their interpretation of the poem. It is interesting that student 'N' waits a long time before asking a question (Q 46). The question appears to be generated from a very active listening stance and is one which could initiate an examination of the sub-text, as suggested earlier in Question 24.

TRAVELING THROUGH THE DARK by W. Stafford	Line number
Traveling through the dark I found a deer.	1
dead on the edge of the Wilson River road.	2
It is usually best to roll them into the canyon:	3
that road is narrow; to swerve might make more dead.	4
By glow of the tail-light I stumbled back of the car	5
and stood by the heap, a doe, a recent killing;	6
she had stiffened already, almost cold.	7
I dragged her off; she was large in the belly.	8
My fingers touching her side brought me the reason—	9
her side was warm; her fawn lay there waiting,	10
alive, still, never to be born.	11
Beside that mountain road I hesitated.	12
The car aimed ahead its lowered parking lights;	13
under the hood purred the steady engine.	14
I stood in the glare of the warm exhaust turning red;	15

> around our group I could hear the wilderness listen.   16
> I thought hard for us all – my only swerving –,   17
> then pushed her over the edge into the river.   18

1 (A1) What made the driver decide to push the dead deer into the river?
2 (B1) Didn't he have to make the road safe for other drivers?
3 (C1) Is this poem really about abortion?
4 (D1) Why do you ask that? Why does it have to be about anything except a car accident?
5 (C2) I didn't say it *had* to. (Statement)
6 (C3) OK. Is it possible that the poem only seems to be about a dead doe but is actually trying to make us think about the *value* of human life?
7 (D2) But it's different, isn't it. If the mother's dead, is it abortion to cause a foetus to die?
8 (E1) Could we shelve the question of abortion so that we can explore other things in the poem?
9 (F1) What else is there? There's no rhyme or anything. (Statement)
10 (F2) Right. Right. So what else is there in this rhymeless poem to talk about?
11 (B2) Isn't the lack of rhyme deliberate?
12 (G1) When the driver gets out of the car, why does he 'stumble'? What makes him stumble?
13 (H1) 'He'?
14 (G1) What do you mean?
15 (H2) Are you just assuming that the driver has to be a guy?
16 (G3) Doesn't the author's name make that pretty clear?
17 (I1) Can't a writer pretend to be someone of the opposite sex?
18 (E2) Wouldn't most people assume, even if the poem wasn't signed, that only a man would have what it takes to push a full-grown pregnant deer over a cliff?
19 (I2) Do you mean physical strength, or lack of sentimentality?
20 (G4) Why 'Or'? Wouldn't it take both kinds of strength – physical and emotional?
21 (H3) Are women more sentimental than men? Isn't that just sexual stereotyping?
22 (G5) OK. Can someone answer why he (or she) stumbles?
23 (H4) Near the end, she (or he) says that thinking about 'us all' was the 'only swerving.' But why is that word used? 'Swerving'? Isn't it like 'stumbling'?
24 (J1) Doesn't 'swerving' just echo 'swerve' in line 4? Is thinking supposed to be dangerous, like driving at night?
25 (K1) Can I just say what I think about all this? Do I have to think of a way to put it into a question?
26 (L1) Why not?

27 (M1) Why?

28 (K2) Well, can I ask several questions at once, so that we don't get sidetracked?

(Pause: everyone waits for a referee to step in. None does.)

29 (K3) OK, here goes. Why is the car described like an animal? And a gun? (pause) If the engine ' purrs' and the car 'aims' its parking lights, is the author making us think that machines are more alive than animals and people?

30 (B2) If cars kill animals sometimes, then isn't it a sensible metaphor to compare a car to a rifle?

31 (H5) And aren't some cars named after animals? Isn't there a Mustang – and a Ram?

32 (B3) And even a cat? A Cougar? Do they purr?

33 (C4) Can we get back to the main point here? I mean, does it really matter if the engine purrs?

34 (B4) What *is* the main point of the poem?

35 (C5) Isn't it whether the driver should have saved the fawn?

36 (B5) Did he have time to do that? What if a car came along?

37 (M2) Can anyone tell me how he could have saved the fawn?

38 (B6) He couldn't, could he?

39 (G6) Couldn't what? Save the fawn? If he couldn't, then what's all this 'hesitating' about?

40 (F3) Yeah. The suspense is all phoney, isn't it? Even if he could cut the fawn out of the doe's belly, it couldn't survive without her, could it?

41 (D3) The poem doesn't say, does it? Isn't it possible for a good vet to save it?

42 (A2) Is the driver a good vet?

43 (K4) Why is the driver 'turning red'? Is he ashamed, or embarrassed or something?

44 (H6) Wouldn't there have to be a comma after 'exhaust' for the driver to be the one turning red? Isn't the 'warm exhaust' turning red in the light from the tail lights'?

45 (K5) Is that ambiguity? Aren't they both turning red?

46 (N1) Can I ask about another word? Does 'still' in line 11 mean 'still born' as well as motionless? If you read the whole line?

(And so the 'quescussion' continues. . . .)

This transcript was part of a workshop handout provided to participants in 'Quescussion' at Brock University, March, 1990 and is included here with permission from Professor Paul M. Bidwell, Department of English, University of Saskatchewan.

Appendix 3

Alternative source for Chapter 12

(Based on Neelands and designed for elementary students by Norah Morgan, who has used it with students in over twenty schools.)

In the year AD 2000 Mary Ellery, daughter of William and Elizabeth Ellery, left her home in Mountsville to travel to the planet Osiris. She was a member of the group 'Venture' led by Dr James Harvey. Mary never returned. The team does not speak of her. There is no mention of her in the records and her name does not appear in the medal citation which honours the work of Dr Harvey and his group.

Notes

2 A QUESTION OF THINKING

1 We are indebted for this example to Carole Tarlington, Artistic Director of the Vancouver Youth Theatre.

4 THE EXAMPLE LESSON: 'SNOW WHITE'

1 This lesson unit was adapted from the plan, notes and assessment made by Linda Laidlaw for a Grade 4 class at Parkdale Community School, Toronto, Ontario. November, 1988.

5 A CLASSIFICATION OF QUESTIONS

1 These categories are taken from and elaborate upon the original classification given in Chapter 4 of Morgan and Saxton (1987).
2 We are unable to trace the publication of this poem, which we have edited for purposes of length. It is, in its entirety, a wonderful piece of material with enormous appeal for students from about age 10 on.

8 FEWER QUESTIONS, BETTER QUESTIONS AND TIME TO THINK

1 'Scaffolding' is Bruner's term for one of the principles of Vygotsky's theory of intellectual development and best describes what it is that goes on when teaching and learning come together in joint activity; that 'zone'where learning is neither 'student-centred' nor 'teacher-centred', but centred in what happens between them; where students' potentials are realized because of teacher guidance and/or collaboration with more capable peers' (Morgan and Saxton, 1989).

12 THE EXAMPLE LESSON: 'ANN GRAHAM'

1 This lesson unit was adapted from a workshop given by Jonothan Neelands in Toronto, October, 1987. He refers to the source as 'a useful case study both of open structure and of the power of student questioning in constructing a narrative'. Neelands' text, *Structuring Drama Work* (Cambridge University Press, 1990), offers other open structures which invite students into active participation in their learning. (For a version of the source which works very well with elementary students, see Appendix 3.)

Bibliography

Allen, Dwight W. (1969) *Questioning Skills* (Teacher's Manual to accompany four film scripts). USA: General Learning.

Ambrosino, Salvatore (Educational Director) (n.d.) *We, the Family: Plays for Living*. Various authors, various dates. New York: Family Service Bureau.

Barnes, Douglas (1976) *The Writer in Australia: a collection of literary documents*. Melbourne: Oxford University Press.

Benjamen, Alfred (1981) *The Helping Interview*. Boston: Houghton Mifflin.

Berlak, A. and Berlak, H. (1987) 'Teachers working with teachers to transform schools', *Educating Teachers: Changing the Nature of Pedagogical Knowledge* (J. Smyth, ed.). Lewes: The Falmer Press: 169–78.

Biehler, Robert F. and Snowman, Jack (1986) *Psychology Applied to Teaching*. (5th edn). Boston: Houghton Mifflin.

Blackburn, Simon (1988) Interview. London: Sunday Observer, 20 November.

Bloom, Benjamin S. and Krathwohl, David R. (1965) *The Taxonomy of Educational Objectives, The Classification of Educational Goals. Handbook 1: Cognitive Domain*. New York: D. McKay.

Bolton, Gavin (1979) *Towards a Theory of Drama in Education*. London: Longman.

Booth, David (1980) *Drama Words*. Toronto: Language Study Centre – Drama.

Bridges, D. (1988) 'A philosophical analysis of discussion', in *Questioning and Discussion: a multidisciplinary study* (J. Dillon, ed.). Norwood, New Jersey: Ablex Publishing, p. 26.

Britton, James (1970) *Language and Learning: The Importance of Speech in Children's Development*. London: Allen Lane.

Browne, M., Neil, K. and Stuart M. (1981) *Asking the Right Questions*. New Jersey: Prentice-Hall.

Brownlie, F., Close, S. and Wingren, L. (1988) 'Request'. *Reaching for higher thought*. Edmonton: Arnold.

Bruner, Jerome (1986) *Actual Minds, Possible Worlds*. Cambridge, Mass.: Harvard University Press.

Cambridge, G. (1949) (ed.) *Bacon's Essays*. London: Oxford University Press.

Creed, Carol L. (1978) 'Purposeful questioning in poetry: guidelines for the classroom'. *Unterrichtspraxis*, 11 (Spring), 12–19.

Dillon, J.T. (1982) 'The effect of questions in education and other enterprises'. *Journal of Curriculum Studies*. 14, 2. 127–52.

Dillon, J.T. (1983) *Teaching and the Art of Questioning*. Bloomington: Phi Delta Kappa Educational Foundation.

Dillon, J.T. (1988a) *Questioning and Discussion: a multidisciplinary study*. Norwood, New Jersey: Ablex Publishing.

Dillon, J.T. (1988b) *Teaching and Questioning: a manual of practice*. London: Croom Helm.
Dressel, Susan (1981) 'The reference base: how to assess the students' meaning'. *Phi Delta Kappan*, February, 457–8.
Duncan, Ronald (n.d.) *Ra*.
Eardley, Anne (1988) 'Questioning'. National Association of Teachers of Drama, *Drama Broadsheet*, 52, 10–14.
Economic Council of Canada (1987) Making technology work: innovation and jobs in Canada. Ottawa: Queen's Printer, Government of Canada.
Edwards, A.E. and Westgate, D.P.G. (1987) *Investigating Classroom Talk*. London and Philadelphia: The Falmer Press, Social Research and Educational Series 4.
Edwards, Derek and Mercer, Neil (1987) *Common Knowledge: The Development of Understanding in the Classroom*. London: Methuen.
Encyclopaedia Britannica (1962) Volume 9. 'Feelings/Emotions' (Harry S. Ashmore, ed.). London: William Benton.
Egan, Kieran (1987) *Teaching as Storytelling*. London, Ontario: Althouse.
Felton, Heather and Stoessiger, Rex (1987) 'Quality learning: the role of process in the arts and mathematics'. National Association of Drama in Education, Australia, *Journal*, 12 (1), 14–22.
Ferrara, Charles L. (1981) 'The joys of leading a discussion'. *English Journal*, 70 (February) 68–71.
Foreman, E.A. and Cazden, C.B. (1985) 'Exploring Vygotskian perspectives in education: the cognitive value of peer interaction', in *Culture, Communication and Cognition: Vygotskian Perspectives*. (J.V. Wertsh, ed.) Cambridge: Cambridge University Press.
Frye, Northrop (1988) *On Education*. Markam, Ontario: Fitzhenry & Whiteside.
Ginsberg, Herbert and Opper, Sylvia (1979) *Piaget's Theory of Intellectual Development*. (2nd edn). London: Prentice-Hall International.
Good, T.L., Salvings, R.L., Harel, K.H. and Emerson, H. (1987) 'Student passivity'. *Sociology of Education*, 60, 181-99.
Grahame, Kenneth (1908) *The Wind in the Willows*. London: Methuen.
Graves, Donald H. (1983) *Writing: Teachers and Children at Work*. Portsmouth, New Hampshire: Heinemann Educational.
Hall, Mr Justice E.M. and Dennis, L.A. (1968) *Living and Learning*. Toronto: Ontario Ministry of Education Publication.
Hannam, Charles, Smyth, Pat and Stephenson, Norman (1977) *Young Teachers and Reluctant Learners*. (revised edn). Harmondsworth: Penguin Books.
Helmore, G.A. (1975) *Piaget: A Practical Consideration*. Oxford: Pergamon.
Holborn, P., Wideen, M. and Andrews, I. (eds) (1987) *Becoming a Teacher*. Toronto: Kagan & Woo.
Holt, John (1973) *Freedom and Beyond*. New York: Dell.
Holt, John (1982) *How Children Fail*. (revised edn). New York: Dell.
Hoover, K.H. and Hollingsworth, P.M. (1978) *A Handbook for Elementary Teachers* (abridged edn). Boston: Allyn & Bacon.
Hunkins, Francis P. (1974) *Questioning Strategies and Techniques*. Boston: Allyn & Bacon.
Improving Teaching in Higher Education, University Teaching Methods Unit (1976) *Asking Questions*. London: Institute of Education, pp. 47–9.
Ivey, Allen E. (1983) *Intentional Interviewing and Counselling*. Monterey, California: Brooks/Cole.
Kelly, George (1963) *Theory of Personality: The Psychology of Personal Constructs*. New York: Norton Library.

Kelly, Trevor (1982) *Effective Questioning: A Teaching Skills Workbook*. London: Macmillan Education (Teacher Education Project).

Kenna, Kathleen (1988) 'Temagami'. *Toronto Star*, 8 December.

Kurfiss, Joanne Gainen (1989) 'Critical thinking by design', *Teaching Excellence: Toward the Best in the Academy*, Autumn. Distributed by The Centre for Teaching Excellence: University of Hawaii at Manoa: 1–2.

Laidlaw, Linda (1989) 'Some further thoughts on questioning'. Toronto (Unpublished).

Laurence, Margaret (1978) *A Bird in the House*. Toronto: Seal Books, McClelland & Stewart.

Lefton, R.E., Buzzotta, K.R. and Shenberg, M. (1980) *Improving Productivity through People Skills*. Mass.: Ballinger, Harper & Row.

Lewis, B. and Pucelik, F. (1982) *Magic Demystified: A Pragmatic Guide to Communication and Change*. Lake Oswego, Oregon: Metamorphosous.

Lindfors, J.W. (1980) *Children's Language and Learning*. New Jersey: Prentice-Hall.

Little, Graham (1983) *Language and Curriculum: A Report prepared for the Language Committee, Tasmanian Education Department*, Australia.

Little, Graham (1984) 'Form follows function: some observations on language, the arts and education'. *NADIE Papers No.1.*, Australia: National Association of Drama in Education.

McGovern, George (1988) Introduction in *How Children Fail* (revised edn), John Holt. New York: Dell.

McKeachie, W.J. (1978) *Starting Discussion with a Question: Teaching Tips: A Guidebook for the Beginning College Teacher*. Mass.: Heath, pp. 38–40.

Malczewski, Carol (1990) 'Towards a theory of ownership in the dramatic process'. Masters thesis, University of Victoria (Unpublished).

Manzo, A.V. (1969) 'The ReQuest Procedure'. Syracuse, NY: International Reading Association, *Journal of Reading*, 13 (2), 123–6.

Marshall, Richard (ed.) (1977) *Great Events of the Twentieth Century*. Canada: Reader's Digest Association.

Maslow, Abraham (1954) *Motivation and Personality* (revised edn). New York: Harper & Row.

Maslow, Abraham (1971) *The Farther Reaches of Human Nature*. New York: Viking.

Maslow, Abraham (1986) *Towards a Psychology of Being*. New York: Van Nostrand.

Michener, James A. (1987) *Legacy*. New York: Fawcett Crest.

Miller, Arthur (1965) *The Crucible*. New York: Viking.

Misher, E.G. (1975) 'Studies in dialogues and discourse: types of discourse initiated and sustained through questioning'. *Journal of Psycholinguistic Research*, 4, 279–305.

Moffett, James and Wagner, Betty Jane (1976) *Student-Centered Language Arts and Reading, K-13: A Handbook for Teachers*. Boston: Houghton Mifflin.

Moore, Kathleen and McEwen, Jessie (1936) *A Picture History of Canada*. Toronto: Nelson.

Morgan, Norah and Saxton, Juliana (1987) *Teaching Drama: a mind of many wonders*. London: Hutchinson.

Morgan, Norah and Saxton, Juliana (1989) 'Not asked for', in *Forum for the Arts and Media Education*, OISE, Toronto, May.

Mussen, Paul H. (ed.) (1983) *Handbook of Child Psychology* (formerly Carmichael's Manual of Child Psychology) Vols 1&2. New York: John Wiley & Sons.

Neelands, J. (1990) *Structuring Drama Work*. Cambridge: Cambridge University Press.

Norman, John (1987) Notes taken from a workshop at the British Council course 'How do you train a drama teacher?', Stanhope, September 6–18.

Norris, Doreen and Boucher, Joyce (1980) *Observing Children through their Formative Years*. Toronto: Board of Education for the City of Toronto.

O'Neill, Cecily (1989) 'Dialogue and drama: the transformation of events, ideas and teachers'. *Language Arts*, 66(2): 147–59.

O'Neil, Cecily and Lambert, Alan (1982) *Drama Structures: A Handbook for Teachers*. London: Hutchinson.

Ontario Ministry of Education (1988) *Science is Happening Here*. Policy statement for science in Primary and Junior Divisions.

Payne, Stanley L. (1951) *The Art of Asking Questions*. USA: Princeton University Press.

Petrie, P.A., Baker, V.E., Derbyshire W., Levitt, J.R., and Maclean W.B. (1953) *Intermediate Mathematics: Book Four*. Toronto: Copp Clarke.

Postman, Neil (1979) *Teaching as a Conserving Activity*. New York: Laurel Press, Dell.

Postman, Neil and Weingartner, Charles (1969) *Teaching as a Subversive Activity*. USA: Delacorte.

Primary English Notes (n.d.). 'Why ask? your guide to good questioning'. Primary Teaching Notes no. 10 prepared by Bruce Cornish (R.D. Walshe, ed.). Australia: Primary English Teaching Association of New South Wales.

Purkey, William (1978) *Inviting School Success: A Self-Concept Approach to Teaching and Learning*. USA: Wadsworth.

'Questioning Techniques' (n.d.) A series of overheads. San Jose, California: Lansford Publishing (ISBN 002 00013305).

Radwanski, George (1987) *Ontario Study of the Relevance of Education and the Issue of Dropouts*. Ontario: Ministry of Education.

Roth, Jason M.A. (n.d.) *Why Can't You Hear What I Haven't Said? : a compilation of writings and thoughts on creative listening and communication*. Halifax, Nova Scotia (no further information available).

Sadker, M. and Sadker, D. (1982) 'Questioning skills' in *Classroom Teaching Skills*, (2nd edn), James M. Cooper (general ed.). Toronto: D.C. Heath, ch. 5.

Sanders, Norris N. (1966) *Classroom Questions: What Kind?* New York: Harper & Row.

Saxton, Juliana and Verriour, Patrick (1988) 'A sense of ownership'. *NADIE Journal*. 12 (2) National Association of Drama in Education, Australia 9–12.

Schaffner, Megan (co-ordinator, Drama and Language Research Project) (1983) *The Power of Drama: A Case Study of Drama in a Primary School*. Tasmania: Speech and Drama Centre.

Smyth, John (ed.) (1987) *Educating Teachers: Changing the Nature of Pedagogical Knowledge*. Philadelphia: The Falmer Press.

Social Studies Curriculum Guide: Grades 8–11 (1988). British Columbia: Curriculum Development Branch, Victoria: Ministry of Education.

Spiegelberg, Herbert (ed.) (1964) *The Socratic Enigma*. USA: Library of Liberal Arts, Bobbs, Merrill.

Stoppard, Tom (1967) *Rosencrantz and Guildenstern are Dead*. London: Samuel French.

Tizard, B. and Hughes, M. (1984) *Young Children Learning: Talking and Thinking at Home and at School*. London: Fontana.

Tough, Joan (1978) *The Development of Meaning*. New York: John Wiley & Sons.

Vygotsky, Lev (1986) *Thought and Language* (revised edn), (A. Kozulin, ed.). Mass.: MIT Press.

Watson, Karilee (1980) 'The Socratic method and levels of questioning'. *College Student Journal*, 14 (Summer), 130–2.

Weingartner, Charles (1977) 'Remedial reasoning'. National Council of Teachers of English, *English Journal*, May, 12–14.

Wells, C. Gordon (1985) *Language Development in the Pre-school Years: Language at Home and at School*. (Vol. 2) Cambridge: Cambridge University Press.

Woods, P. (ed.) (1980) *Pupil Strategies*. London: Croom Helm.

Woods, P. (1987) 'Life histories and teacher knowledge', in *Educating Teachers: Changing the Nature of Pedagogical Knowledge* (J. Smyth, ed.). Lewes: The Falmer Press, pp. 121–35.

Woods, P. and Hammersley, M. (eds) (1977) *School Experience*. London: Croom Helm.

Index

Asking Better Questions
Models, techniques and activities
for engaging students in learning

We learn by asking questions. We learn better by asking better questions. We learn more by having opportunities to ask more questions. The aim of this book is to help both teachers and students develop their questioning skills in order to share in the process of inquiry.

Asking Better Questions offers teachers practical suggestions, illustrated with examples from classroom experience, based upon current educational thinking, and springing from a sound philosophical stance. Part I sets out the reasons for the limited effectiveness of questions in present classroom practice, and examines the two structures which form the matrix of all educational processes: the structure for thinking and the structure for feeling. Part II looks at a simple three-part classification of general functions for questions: those which tap into what is already known and which elicit a sense of responsibility towards the conduct of, and approach to, the work; those which build a context for shared understanding; and those which challenge students to think critically and creatively for themselves. Part III looks at classroom discourse and the techniques which promote an environment for talk. It focuses on building questioning skills for teachers and students, suggesting techniques for posing questions and dealing with answers.

The authors have between them over fifty years of classroom experience at the primary, secondary and post-secondary level. Their book *Teaching Drama: A Mind of Many Wonders* has been adopted on education courses in Canada, the United States, Great Britain and Australia. **Norah Morgan** is Adjunct Professor with the Faculty of Education, Brock University, Ontario. **Juliana Saxton** is responsible for the Drama and Theatre in Education Programme at the University of Victoria, British Columbia.